The

POWER
of
CHARACTER in
LEADERSHIP

The
POWER
of
CHARACTER in
LEADERSHIP

DR. MYLES
MUNROE

W
WHITAKER
HOUSE

THE POWER OF CHARACTER IN LEADERSHIP:
How Values, Morals, Ethics, and Principles Affect Leaders

Dr. Myles Munroe
Bahamas Faith Ministries International
P.O. Box N9583
Nassau, Bahamas
bfmadmin@bfmmm.com
www.bfmmm.com; www.bfmi.tv; www.mylesmunroe.tv

Hardcover ISBN: 978-1-60374-954-1 • Trade paperback edition ISBN: 978-1-60374-955-8
eBook ISBN: 978-1-60374-979-4
Printed in the United States of America
© 2014 by Myles Munroe

Whitaker House
1030 Hunt Valley Circle
New Kensington, PA 15068
www.whitakerhouse.com

Library of Congress Cataloging-in-Publication Data (Pending)

1 2 3 4 5 6 7 8 9 10 11 12 13 **UJ** 23 22 21 20 19 18 17 16 15 14

Preface

The most valuable component of leadership is not power, position, influence, notoriety, fame, talent, gifting, dynamic oratory, persuasiveness, intellectual superiority, academic achievement, or management skills. It is *character*. Character is the cradle of credibility for the leader. Without the element of strong, noble, honorable character, leadership and all its potential achievements are in danger of cancellation. Every leader is only as safe and secure as his character.

I offer this book as a resource on this often-neglected aspect of leadership, which is personal but also extremely practical. Having a foundation of ethics is central to the success and longevity of one's leadership.

Many leadership training seminars and academic programs focus on vision, skills, management, organization, teamwork, and many other helpful subjects. Yet few of these courses address the topic of the leader's character. The subject is either downplayed or never covered at all. This oversight is tragic. Not only has it permitted the encroachment of an unhealthy atmosphere of negative attitudes and practices among leaders, but it has also led to destructive consequences for individuals, societies, and nations.

Character is the most powerful force a leader can cultivate because it protects leadership. It will enable you to be a success, personally and professionally, as you carry out your purpose, vision, and goals in life.

The Power of Character in Leadership is for...

+ **Leaders who are currently pursuing a vocational calling and desire to be the very best they can be.** You will learn how to establish yourself solidly as a leader and reach your goals as you cultivate enduring influence.

- *Those who are emerging leaders or who aspire to lead.* You will discover how ethics and values free you to carry out your singular purpose in life.

- *Leaders who have failed—perhaps in a major way—due to a character flaw of some kind.* You are probably asking yourself, "How did I get to this place? What do I do now? Do I still have a future as a leader?" You will see how to rebuild the foundation of your life. Ethically, you may be on shaky ground right now, but you can begin the process of developing a renewed mind-set and a solid code of ethics that will lead to sound moral character. If you've fallen, this book explains how to "fall up" by making changes that will transform you from the inside out.

- *Anyone who is concerned about the lack of moral force in leadership today.* Having leaders of character on the local, national, and global levels is the key to solving a myriad of problems in our world. This book reveals a process for rebuilding our leaders so they can tackle the issues of our day.

- *People who don't yet understand that they are leaders.* If you believe that leadership is for only a select few, you have accepted a false idea about leaders. Every person on earth is a leader in a particular area of gifting—and character development provides the foundation for discovering how you were born to lead.

In relation to the last point, the focus of my leadership training has always been the transformation of followers into leaders, and leaders into agents of change. There are millions of people who have tremendous potential for leadership, but no one has ever encouraged them to express it and develop it. In fact, many people are being told that they are "nothing." Eventually, they believe it, so they do not fulfill their purpose in life.

If that has been your perspective, this book will help you to understand what it means to be a genuine leader and how to develop your leadership potential.

Regardless of your background, I invite you to discover the remarkable power of character in leadership—and how values, morals, ethics, and principles affect both the development and the outcome of your personal leadership success.

Contents

Introduction: Contemporary Leadership and the Crisis of Character......9

Part I: The Priority of Character

1. Character Matters 29
2. Leaders of Conviction 47

Part II: The Source of Moral Leadership

3. How Character Develops, Part I: What We Believe 69
4. How Character Develops, Part II: What We Value..........81
5. How Character Develops, Part III: What We Serve.........99
6. The Role of Values in Corporate Life....................113
7. The Origin of Our Moral Conscience.....................135
8. The Power of Principles 157

Part III: Personal Character Development

9. Key Concepts of Character 173
10. Tempting Your Character................................187
11. Core Qualities of Principled Leaders...................203

Part IV: Restoring a Culture of Character

12. Integrating Vision and Values 215

How to "Fall Up": Restoration After Character Failure 227

Notes..230

Character Development Worksheets...........................238

About the Author...251

Introduction

Contemporary Leadership and the Crisis of Character

"Whatever failures I have known, whatever errors I have committed, whatever follies I have witnessed in public and private life have been the consequences of action without thought."
—Bernard Baruch, businessman and advisor to U.S. presidents

In the dynamic drama of contemporary leadership playing on the world stage today, there are many "characters" who lack character. Moreover, the trail of history is littered with many would-be great men and women who harnessed the reins of power in various fields—political, social, economic, corporate, athletic, spiritual, and more. They wielded great influence and/or control over the lives of others; many felt the weight of material wealth and fame—only to have it all disintegrate and blow away like dust in the wind because of their tragic deficiencies of character.

A lack of strong leadership has made a mess of our world. Every country on earth is challenged by an absence of resolute leadership as it struggles under precarious times. Politically, economically, and socially, our nations are experiencing turmoil and moral decay—characterized by crime, religious conflicts, economic uncertainty, the unequal distribution of resources, political corruption, civil unrest, the disintegration of the family, cybercrime, poverty, disease, famine, sexual abuse, greed, racial clashes, ethnic "cleansing," global terrorism, and war.

Our twenty-first century world seems to be an experiment in global self-destruction. We need strong leaders who have the courage to grapple with perplexing issues and seemingly overwhelming problems, as well as the ability to discover and implement workable solutions. More than anything else, what we require today are competent, effective, visionary leaders in all walks of life.

The Missing Element: "Moral Force"

The leaders who have emerged today seem to believe that the primary qualities needed to address our troubled, demanding times are the following: great vision; academic and intellectual superiority; dynamic oratory and other communications skills that have the power to persuade; management expertise; and the ability to control others. However, time and again, history has shown that the most important quality a true leader should and must possess is the moral force of a noble and stable character.

There are about two hundred countries in the world today, and each one has leaders on the national, regional, and local level. Many nations also have aspiring leaders who run for public office each year. In addition, corporations and businesses, religious institutions, nonprofit organizations and community groups, and other enterprises in society all have leaders. Many people, in a variety of fields—economics, government, law, business, education, medicine, science, entertainment, sports, and so forth—are leaders or are training to be leaders.

We have all these skilled people in positions of power, with an ample supply of potential leaders. Yet the leaders who are trying to keep their nations, companies, organizations, and families from sinking are either lacking, or deficient in, that vital element of character.

Across the globe, we have seen leaders fall apart, ethically and morally. Many leaders start strong (or appear to), only to end up "crashing and burning." A number of leaders have operated under a reputation of integrity that was only a façade. While they appeared competent and well-adjusted on the outside, they lacked real substance within. They were missing the element of moral force, and their ethical poverty eventually became evident. The public didn't know who these leaders really were—until the leaders became enmeshed in scandal due to their reckless conduct, often finding themselves facing legal consequences for unlawful financial practices, theft, extortion, cheating, perjury...and the like.

*The public didn't know who their leaders really were—until the
leaders became enmeshed in scandal.*

Meanwhile, other people in positions of power have been hindered by
incompetence because they have never learned solid leadership principles
and how to implement them. Others are capable, but they still aren't helping to address the needs of their society because they would rather destroy
a corporate competitor or nullify a political opponent than work together
with other leaders to address serious problems and find solutions.

Leadership Is Central in Our World

The contemporary crisis of character in leadership is alarming because,
to a great extent, leaders determine the direction, security, and prosperity
of cultures, societies, and nations. The following concepts demonstrate the
central role of leadership in human society.

+ **Nothing happens without leadership.** Leaders establish governments, start businesses, make scientific discoveries and advances,
  disseminate religious and philosophical ideas, and otherwise foster
  human culture.

+ **Nothing succeeds without leadership.** Leaders develop ideas,
  carry out endeavors, and keep projects going.

+ **Nothing is altered or transformed without leadership.** Unless
  an individual or a group of people begin to think differently or act
  differently, circumstances usually remain the same—or become
  worse.

+ **Nothing develops without leadership.** Leaders take initiative to
  implement innovations, build on what has come before, and expand
  on prior successes.

+ **Nothing advances without leadership.** Leaders are enterprising
  and forward-looking. They are often eager to enhance a society's
  quality of life through improved efficiency, greater convenience,
  and the introduction of new products and services.

- **Nothing improves without leadership.** Leaders see potential in situations and conditions where others see no hope and have no vision of the way things *could be.*

- **Nothing is corrected without leadership.** To fix errors and solve problems, someone has to take responsibility to see that adjustments are made. Leaders help societies to make a course correction when they have veered onto a destructive path.

Leadership is therefore key to human preservation, growth, and change. No matter what condition a society or nation finds itself in, it didn't arrive there by accident. Someone led them there.

Every person on earth is being guided, influenced, or manipulated by someone. Directly or indirectly, consciously or unconsciously, we are continually being led by those who are our "official" leaders, as well as those who have become our de facto leaders by their influence over us. That is why our current problems won't be solved without a renewed emphasis on the foundational elements of positive and effective leadership. Countries, corporations, institutions, organizations, departments, and so forth will be effective and successful only insofar as their leaders are effective and successful. When leaders in all realms of life make a commitment to strengthen their leadership, they will enable their society to improve, survive, and progress.

> *"We know that leadership is very much related to change.*
> *As the pace of change accelerates, there is naturally a*
> *greater need for effective leadership."*
> **—John Kotter, renowned businessman, professor, and author**

Who Has Been Leading Us?

I have spoken at universities where I've met administrators, professors, and students. I have been a consultant to corporate gurus and government leaders. I have been interviewed on hundreds of television shows. In the process, I have met many well-known leaders. Yet, with a few exceptions, the famous and influential people I have encountered have not impressed me with their leadership because it did not appear to include the essential ingredient of character.

Who has been leading our nations? Unfortunately, we have been influenced by many leaders and institutions that lack the quality of moral force—and their attitudes and actions are being absorbed by the culture at large.

Below is a sampling of leaders and organizations in various realms of life that, at the time of the writing of this manuscript, have been associated with ethical controversies, sexual and financial scandals, or criminal activity. In essence, they were victims of our society's crisis of defective character. Many leaders on the world and national stage who should be about the business of building up their nations are instead violating the public trust, breaking the law, and committing crimes against humanity. They are finding themselves in the headlines—and appearing before judges and other tribunals.

Some of the issues represented in this list are complex, while others are straightforward. At the time this book went to press, the outcomes of several of these situations were yet to be resolved—either by legislatures or courts. In some cases, not all the facts have been made public to allow for a full assessment. Yet these examples from the last several decades illustrate the range of ethical and moral crises in leadership with which the United States and nations around the world are being confronted.

Government and Politics

+ The administration of U.S. President Barack Obama is dealing with several controversial ethical issues. Mr. Obama was admonished by the press, members of the U.S. Congress, and the public regarding the Justice Department's subpoenas of the phone records of reporters from the Associated Press while the department gathered intelligence related to a leak about a terrorist threat. A similar controversy flared in relation to phone records from Fox News in regard to Justice's investigation into a leak about North Korea.[1] Likewise, the president came under fire for the National Security Agency's ongoing practice of monitoring the phone records of ordinary Americans while looking for possible terrorist activity.[2] In addition, the White House was criticized after revelations that the Internal Revenue Service (IRS) gave certain conservative groups extra scrutiny when they applied for tax-exempt status. All of these issues are ongoing.

+ Anthony Weiner of New York resigned his seat in the U.S. Congress after it was disclosed that the married congressman had sent sexually explicit text messages and photographs to women. He then ran for mayor of New York City, refusing to drop out of the primary race, even after a subsequent "sexting" scandal, despite political pressure to do so.

+ President Bill Clinton was impeached by the U.S. House of Representatives for perjury and obstruction of justice related to his testimony about the Monica Lewinsky scandal. He remained in office when the impeachment votes for both charges failed in the Senate.

+ Ronald Reagan's presidency was tainted by the Iran-Contra affair, in which the National Security Agency sold arms to Iran in exchange for American hostages, even though an embargo against Iran was in effect. Some of the money from the sale then went to Nicaraguan "Contras" to support their fight against the Sandinista government. This was in violation of the Boland Amendment, which was passed by Congress to prohibit military aid to the Contras. National Security Advisor Rear Admiral John Poindexter resigned, and charges were filed against fourteen people, though six were later pardoned by President George H. W. Bush.[3]

+ Richard Nixon became the first U.S. president to resign his office in the wake of his participation in a cover-up of illegal activities authorized by members of his staff during his reelection campaign. The year prior to Nixon's resignation, his vice president resigned his office due to political corruption involving bribery and extortion, as well as tax evasion.

+ The former president of Brazil, Luiz Inacio Lula da Silva, is being investigated for his alleged role in a scheme to buy votes from members of the Brazilian Congress during the time he was in office.[4]

+ The newly elected president of Kenya and his deputy president, William Ruto, face trial by the International Criminal Court for "crimes against humanity, including murder and rape."[5] The *Wall Street Journal* reported, "The court alleges Mr. Kenyatta and his deputy president, William Ruto, incited gang violence that left more than 1,000 people dead following his predecessor's disputed election in 2007. Both men deny the charges."[6]

+ The Yugoslav war crimes tribunal of the United Nations "convicted six Bosnian Croat political and military leaders...of persecuting, expelling, and murdering Muslims during Bosnia's war." The convictions may be appealed.[7]

+ Manuel Noriega, the former dictator of Panama, served a prison sentence of almost two decades in the United States for drug trafficking. He then served a brief time in jail in France for money laundering and was required to surrender nearly three million dollars held in his French bank accounts. France then permitted that he be extradited to Panama to serve prison time there for murder.[8]

Business and Economics

+ JPMorgan Chase & Co. agreed to pay $410 million in response to charges of price manipulation: "The bank's energy unit, JP Morgan Venture Energy Corporation, was accused of raising electricity rates in [California and Midwest] markets between September 2010 and November 2012 through 'manipulative bidding strategies,' according to the Federal Energy Regulatory Commission."[9] Previously, the company lost $7 billion after it "engaged in risky trades (derivatives)." This loss had led to various investigations into the company's practices and procedures.[10]

+ Employees at Halliburton, the contractor for British Petroleum (BP) in the Deepwater Horizon oil well project, destroyed evidence concerning the 2010 explosion and massive oil spill in the Gulf of Mexico that killed eleven people. Under a plea bargain, the U.S. Department of Justice charged the company with a misdemeanor, fined it $200,000, gave it three years' probation, and required that the company cooperate with the department's ongoing investigation of the Deepwater incident.[11] Halliburton has been involved in other ethical controversies, including the charge by the Securities and Exchange Commission that the subsidiary of a company owned by Halliburton "bribed Nigerian government officials over a 10-year period, in violation of the Foreign Corrupt Practices Act (FCPA)."[12]

+ In the Deepwater incident, "BP agreed to pay $4.5 billion in penalties and pleaded guilty to 14 criminal charges related to the explosion."[13] The company apparently ignored advice from the Halliburton engineer to install a safer pipe and failed to test the cement sealing to see if it had been successful.[14]

+ Former Wall Street mogul Bernie Madoff operated "the biggest Ponzi scheme in history...[he] bilked his clients of billions of dollars and fooled regulators for decades...."[15] Madoff was convicted of securities fraud, investment advisor fraud, wire and mail fraud, money laundering, filing false documents with the Securities and Exchange Commission, making false statements, perjury, and theft from employee benefit funds. He was sentenced to 150 years in prison.[16]

+ Over the course of decades, the Vatican Bank has been decried and investigated for functioning according to an internal culture of corruption, including alleged money laundering and ties with the Mafia. In 2013, there was a shakeup of leadership at the bank after a new money laundering scandal.[17]

+ The former chairman of the mammoth Hong Kong-based Carrian Group received a three-year sentence for bribing bank officials to obtain loans the equivalent of $238 million in U.S. dollars.[18]

+ The German company Siemons agreed to a settlement of €330 million with the Greek government for alleged bribery in connection with contract bids for the 2004 Olympic Games in Athens.[19]

+ Among other companies involved in child labor scandals, the clothing company GAP released a report in 2004 in which they acknowledged breaches of child labor laws and workplace safety.[20]

+ Through revelations by former tobacco executive and whistleblower Jeffrey Wigand, it was disclosed that cigarette companies like Brown & Williamson had been intentionally attempting to addict consumers to nicotine.[21]

Sports

+ The spotless public image of golf champion Tiger Woods was tarnished when his multiple extramarital affairs became public. His wife divorced him, and he lost several lucrative endorsement deals worth $100 million. Woods received therapy for sexual addiction and returned to the sport.[22]

+ In 2007, New England Patriots coach Bill Belichick was fined $500,000 and the team was fined $250,000 in the so-called Spygate scandal involving the videotaping of opposing teams' coaching signals. The Patriots also had to forgo a potential first-round draft pick.

+ Champion cyclist Lance Armstrong and Olympic sprinter Marion Jones are among many athletes who have admitted to using illegal performance-enhancing drugs. Armstrong's seven Tour de France titles were taken away, and he was banned from professional cycling for life.[23] Jones was stripped of her three Olympic gold medals and sentenced to six months in prison, two years' probation, and community service for lying about her drug use to a federal agent, as well as for her participation in a check fraud operation.[24]

+ Jerry Sandusky, former assistant football coach at Penn State University, received a thirty- to sixty-year prison sentence after being convicted of 45 counts of child sexual abuse.[25]

+ Baseball star Pete Rose, a former Cincinnati Reds player and manager, was indicted for repeated gambling on baseball games and was banned from baseball for life. He also served five months of jail time and community service for income tax evasion.[26]

Religion

+ Numerous sexual abuse allegations have been lodged against Catholic priests in nations around the world. Charges have been filed in various cases, and there has been fallout over cover-ups and inaction by Church officials.[27]

+ Atlanta megachurch pastor Bishop Eddie Long was accused of sexually abusing four teens. Bishop Long has stated that he is innocent, and he settled out of court with the plaintiffs.[28] Concerning a separate case, twelve former church members filed a lawsuit against Long and financial adviser Ephren W. Taylor for losses in an alleged Ponzi scheme.[29] The Securities and Exchange Commission has filed a lawsuit over the scheme in U.S. District Court against Taylor, his company, and his former chief operating officer.[30]

+ Once-prominent televangelist Jimmy Swaggart lost credibility and influence when he became enmeshed in a sex scandal involving a prostitute.[31] Televangelist Jim Bakker was also caught up in a scandal due to his adulterous relationship with a former church secretary. In addition, he spent time in prison for mail and wire fraud and conspiracy in relation to his ministry's fund-raising.[32]

+ Ted Haggard resigned as pastor of his church in Colorado and as president of the National Association of Evangelicals after a homosexual affair with a male prostitute, as well as illegal drug use.[33]

Arts, Entertainment, and Media

+ Mel Gibson, formerly one of Hollywood's most popular and influential actors, was divorced by his wife after more than thirty years of marriage and seven children, for "irreconcilable differences," though infidelity may have played a role; his wife was awarded half his fortune.[34] Gibson was also convicted of hitting his girlfriend, resulting in a sentence of three years' probation, counseling, and community service.[35]

+ *New York Times* reporter Jayson Blair was fired for unethical reporting. The *Times'* public editor, Margaret Sullivan, stated that Blair "lied and faked and cheated his way through story after story—scores of them, for years. He fabricated sources, plagiarized material from other publications, and pretended to be places he never went." The reporter's conduct hurt the *Times'* reputation for accuracy and honesty.[36]

+ Author James Frey admitted to fabricating facts in his best-selling memoir *A Million Little Pieces*, setting off a controversy about what constitutes memoir and the line between fact and fiction.[37]

+ Singing superstar Whitney Houston died tragically of accidental drowning when she was in the midst of a professional comeback, with "the effects of heart disease and cocaine found in her system… contributing factors."[38]

Charity/Nonprofit

+ Greg Mortenson, coauthor of the best-selling book *Three Cups of Tea: One Man's Mission to Promote Peace One School at a Time*, was cited for mismanagement of his charity Central Asia Institute, as well as the misuse of funds. The attorney general of Montana, where the charity is located, stated, "Mr. Mortenson may not have intentionally deceived the board or his employees, but his disregard for and attitude about basic record keeping and accounting for his activities essentially had the same effect." Mortenson was not charged with any criminal activity, and he agreed to repay $1 million to the charity.[39]

+ *Three Cups of Tea* describes Mortenson's humanitarian work in Pakistan and Afghanistan. The book was coauthored by David Oliver Relin. In a controversy unrelated to the charity mismanagement, there were allegations that Mortenson had included fabrications in his book, while Mortenson asserted only some literary license was taken. Coauthor Relin, whose integrity was effectively never in question in the matter, had acknowledged in his introduction to the book that there might be unavoidable inaccuracies in relating Mortenson's experiences. He wrote, "His fluid sense of time made pinning down the exact sequence of many events in this book almost impossible."[40] The controversy placed stress on Relin vocationally, as well as financially, as he defended himself in a civil lawsuit over the book that was brought against Mortenson and himself. A judge dismissed the suit. Relin committed suicide in 2012; his family stated that he had "suffered from depression."[41]

- The former head of the United Way, William Aramony, spent six years in prison for his part in embezzling between $600,000 and $1.2 million from the charitable agency. He used the money to support a "lavish lifestyle" and a young mistress.[42] Aramony was convicted of "among other things, conspiracy to defraud, mail fraud, wire fraud, transportation of fraudulently acquired property, engaging in monetary transactions in unlawful activity, filing false tax returns, and aiding in the filing of false tax returns."[43]

- The charitable organization Feed the Children fired its founder and director, Larry Jones, for alleged misconduct. Jones filed a wrongful-termination lawsuit, and the organization filed a countersuit, "accus[ing] Jones of taking bribes, hoarding hardcore pornography...using a charity employee as a personal nanny...misspending charity funds, pocketing travel money, and keeping gifts from appearances."[44] Jones maintains his innocence. He and Feed the Children reached an out-of-court settlement in which Jones apparently received some compensation but was not reinstated as head of the organization.[45]

These are some examples of public figures, companies, and government agencies that have been associated with issues and scandals involving character, ethics, and the violation of the law. Many more examples could be cited. Revelations of such scandals have become commonplace—they are reported almost every day in newspapers, on broadcast and cable news, on the Internet, on Facebook, and via Twitter.

From a leadership standpoint, these situations illustrate several realities: (1) Character problems are widespread among leaders in many fields of endeavor. (2) A leader's character flaws often end up hurting innocent people. (3) No matter how many accomplishments a leader achieves, no matter how much money he makes, and no matter how high he goes up the ladder of success, if he is deficient in character, his talent and skill are no guarantee he will stay on top, or that he won't pay a great price.

Ask Bill Clinton. Ask Bernie Madoff. Ask Lance Armstrong. Ask Jim Bakker. Ask Mel Gibson. Ask Greg Mortenson. Their character flaws caught up with them. For some, it tainted their reputations. For others, it virtually destroyed their lives, as well as the lives of others. For this reason, the critical issue of character must be addressed, as nations, regions, and local communities; businesses and corporations; civic organizations; religious groups; political parties; armed forces; educational institutions; and families continue to search for quality and qualified leaders to take the helm of responsibility and guide them to a better life and a promising future.

Though the above are high-profile cases that became national and global scandals, the disintegration of character today is found in every type of leadership and on every level of society—including the local level and "ordinary" people's lives. It is found in our homes, with leaders (spouses and parents) who have extramarital affairs, use illegal drugs, abuse alcohol, rack up gambling debts, enter into risky financial investments in hopes of finding a fast track to wealth, abuse family members, and engage in other destructive actions. It is found in our local companies, with workers who embezzle money, steal equipment, or are lazy on the job. It is found in our schools, with teachers who engage in sexual relations with their students, or with students who cheat on exams and engage in bullying through social networks—and sometimes even bring guns to school and shoot their classmates and teachers. It is found in our universities, with professors who plagiarize scholarly works and undergraduates who pay other students to write their term papers.

No one should think he is too smart or too safe to avoid consequences of a lack of character.

Perhaps you are thinking, *I'm not in danger of losing my job or being sentenced to prison.* However, if we as leaders ignore the necessity of character development—if we allow character defects to influence us—we risk failure in our personal lives, our leadership, and our future. No one should think he is too smart or too safe to avoid consequences of a lack of character.

A Psyche of Distrust

One disturbing result of the crisis of character in leadership is that it has created a psyche of distrust among the general public. There are, of course, many earnest, hardworking people of integrity in all walks of life who strive to do the right thing and are helping to uphold the society in which they live. But while the nations of the world desperately need strong, authentic leaders, too many people in positions of authority are self-absorbed. They operate according to misplaced priorities or opportunistic motives. They fail to offer anything of lasting value to their families, associates, clients, customers, or fellow citizens. Instead, they abuse and misuse them. Ethically deficient leaders are leaving a legacy of fear, skepticism, and confusion among those who follow them or are otherwise affected by their leadership.

For example, will the time come when we can watch a race at a track-and-field meet or a cycling event and not secretly ask ourselves if the champion won because he used performance-enhancing drugs? We often harbor the notion that the winner must have cheated somehow. Or, even though we may make allowance for some unintended memory lapses, when will we be able to read a memoir and not have to wonder if some or most of it has been fabricated? Sadly, we have become wary of the validity of such accounts. Or again, when a large corporation is successful, when will we be rid of lingering suspicions about its business practices and how it turned a profit? We question whether big corporations can make money and still be ethical.

What Happened to Character in Leadership?

Why are today's leaders so deficient in character? A major reason is that, across the globe, much of leadership training—both formal and informal—fails to emphasize or even include the concept of character as an essential element of leadership. In addition, many governmental and corporate leaders, along with supervisors, bosses, and others in authority, are not mentoring their colleagues and employees in important principles of character development (though they still expect honesty and integrity from them). Instead, as we will see, other elements of leadership have been given priority—titles, position, power, intelligence, skills, gifts, talents, educational qualifications, knowledge, competence, and charisma or other personality traits.

In the process, we have produced...

+ charismatic leaders without character

+ gifted leaders without convictions

+ powerful leaders without principles

+ intellectual leaders without morality

+ visionary leaders without values

+ spiritual leaders without conscience

The nations of the world do not lack people in leadership positions. They lack genuine leadership *in* their leaders. The result is that we have no shortage of individuals running our countries and businesses and organizations who have titles and high-level positions. They are well-dressed and well-groomed. They are excellent communicators. They are highly skilled in their fields. Yet, as we have noted, these qualities haven't prevented an epidemic of "character fallout" among leaders of various categories— whether presidents and prime ministers, CEOs and directors, priests and pastors, or spouses and parents.

The nations of the world do not lack people in leadership positions. They lack genuine leadership in their leaders.

Telltale Signs

What great leaders can you name who are alive today? (If you weren't able to answer that question without giving it a lot of thought, you're not alone.)

As I write this, Nelson Mandela has been in the hospital for two months due to a lung infection. Mandela was the first democratically elected leader of South Africa and was instrumental in dismantling apartheid. He is now in his mid-nineties. Over the past few years, I have noticed that every time he is admitted to the hospital, people around the world hold their breaths, because no one knows how much longer he will be with us.

What is it about our image of this man that makes us afraid to lose him, even though we understand he is at an advanced age? Could it be that we do not want Mr. Mandela to die because he may be one of the last remaining bastions of true leadership—a man who stands as the definition of character, which we all personally long for and want to see evidenced in the leaders we desire to follow? Is he among the last in a line of historical figures who possessed a vital leadership quality that has very little to do with standard ideas of "power" but nevertheless has the ability to change the world?

I believe that Nelson Mandela's strong convictions about human dignity and equality among the races are the reason people all over the world want him to live forever. Perhaps South Africans are afraid their country might fall apart after he passes. To me, people's anxious reactions to the health of Mr. Mandela, aside from being expressions of human compassion and respect, are telltale signs that character in leadership is so rare that people feel we can't afford to let go of one great leader.

The Future of Leadership

What will be the future of leadership in our world? A familiar but significant truth applies to our present leadership crisis: You can lead people only as far as you have gone yourself. And many of our leaders have not stepped up to the starting line of character development, let alone crossed over it.

Many well-known people who have failed ethically have issued apologies through the media. Even though admitting you were wrong (or that you "made a mistake") and saying you are sorry is a good start, if it is heartfelt, it doesn't necessarily indicate a resolve to change your behavior and act responsibly in the future. You have to make a personal commitment to do that. You have to allow it to become an internal conviction—part of your personal code of ethics.

A future that includes strong, ethical leaders in our governments, businesses, educational institutions, civil organizations, and homes will be secured only by a return to character training and personal character development as our *priority*. Leaders must embrace this challenge and actively seek to change their ways if our nations are to move from a mind-set of corruption and compromise to an outlook of conviction and character. Instead of seeking political power or economic power or entertainment power or sports power, leaders should pursue political character or economic character or entertainment character or sports character.

A future that includes strong, ethical leaders will be secured only by a return to character training and personal character development as our priority.

A new type of leader must begin to emerge within our governing institutions, our communities, our businesses, our places of employment, our families—and ourselves. Leadership that is weak in ethics and values has allowed our nations to fall apart. It has also initiated many of the problems we grapple with in the world. A return to character in leadership will enable us to begin to address these problems from a position of strength, resolve, and honor.

I have given talks on the power of character in leadership in various halls of government across the globe. Some leaders have literally wept as they've explained that no one has ever taught them about the part character plays in leadership. They were instructed on how to manage resources, but they were never taught how to manage their own lives—and how their application of such knowledge was crucial for effective and successful leadership.

Each of us must not only understand and implement the principles of leadership but also make a commitment to become established in character, adhering to a strong code of ethics. Then we must continually grow in the development of our character, so that we can have a positive and lasting impact on our generation and generations to come.

"A sum can be put right: but only by going back till you find the error and working it afresh from that point, never by simply going on."[46]
—C. S. Lewis

PART I:

The Priority of Character

1

Character Matters

"A man's character is his fate."
—Heraclitus, Greek philosopher

On the day that former business magnate Bernard Madoff was sentenced to 150 years in prison for his massive Ponzi scheme—which cost his clients billions of dollars—the judge made some striking comments about Madoff's life and leadership:

> In terms of mitigating factors in a white-collar fraud case such as this, I would expect to see letters from family and friends and colleagues. But not a single letter has been submitted attesting to Mr. Madoff's good deeds or good character or civic or charitable activities. The absence of such support is telling.[1]

Remarkably—and significantly—not one friend, family member, neighbor, colleague, or acquaintance came forward to offer a positive statement about Madoff's character or deeds. Such a statement might have helped to commute his sentence, allowing him the possibility of being released on bail some time before the end of his life.

"Better than Gold"

An ancient proverb declares, "A good name is more desirable than great riches; to be esteemed is better than silver or gold."[2] Many fallen leaders could affirm the truth of this proverb. While some have fallen from higher and more public places than others, they have all suffered losses. These losses were avoidable, but they came about because the leaders lacked "a good name," or integrity.

Starting Strong Then Self-destructing

I have been training leaders for more than thirty years, in more than seventy nations. It has been a true joy to see men and women throughout the world discover who they were born to be, and subsequently make an impact on their homes, communities, businesses, and nations through their personal leadership.

There's nothing I want more than for leaders to be successful—fulfilling their purpose and vision in life. Specifically, I want *you*, as a leader, to succeed.

Yet I have observed a troubling development in our world. Too many leaders start strong but then fail or self-destruct because of defects in their moral compass. As a result, they lose much—or all—they have worked for. They nullify their potential, so that they are unable to make future contributions to their generation. And *every* leader's contribution is needed today as we face a myriad of complicated issues and crises across the globe that need the influence of strong leadership. This is a critical time in our world when the future of leadership is at stake.

The Greatest Obstacle to Leadership Success

As a leadership consultant, I have witnessed the frustrations of national leaders and their cabinet ministers as they have tried to deal with the complex political, economic, and social challenges confronting their nations. I have worked with corporate executives who were determined to discover a more principled and effective leadership approach for themselves and their staff members. I have observed the string of fallen leaders in a variety of fields whose ethical failings have been shouted to the world almost daily via news headlines and talk show programs.

Everywhere, people are struggling with the idea of what it means to be a leader and on what foundation they can build true leadership.

> *This is a critical time in our world when
> the future of leadership is at stake.*

Certainly, there are times when a leader fails because his knowledge and skills aren't right for the particular business, organization, or government for which he works. Or, the timing may not be right for him—perhaps he was promoted too soon and isn't able to handle the responsibility. It could be that his lack of training in the essential principles of leadership keeps him from pursuing his purpose and potential, or from recognizing the right time to move to the next level of leadership. In such cases, the person's position is not one that can—or should—be preserved. He needs to step back and reevaluate his true place as a leader.

Yet I have concluded that the greatest obstacle to a leader's success is a deficit of character. If I could teach a leader one thing that I believe would preserve his leadership, and even his very life, it would be the priority of character—internal values and principles that one is committed to and that manifest in one's life as ethical conduct.

What Kind of Character?

Throughout this book, we will be examining various definitions of character so that we may have a full picture of its meanings and applications. We'll begin with one of the most universal. Character is:

the complex of mental and ethical traits marking and often individualizing a person, group, or nation.

In the sense of this definition, everyone has "character." We are each identified by the sum of our mental and ethical traits.

But the question we are asking is this: As we exercise leadership, of what kind, or quality, are our mental and ethical traits? Are they positive or negative? Do they build up or tear down? As we talk about character, therefore, we will focus on what it means to develop and manifest honorable principles and ethics that will distinguish our lives.

In the world of leadership training, there is an abundance of seminars and workshops that offer instruction on the leader's purpose, vision, and passion. There are also many academic courses available on leadership principles, business management, team building, and so forth. While important, they focus mainly on the mechanics of leadership.

How many courses or training sessions do you see offered on the topic of character formation and the establishment of strong values? On how to live according to one's conscience, not compromising one's standards? Not many. This vital aspect of leadership is being overlooked—to our own detriment.

Moral deficits frequently lead people to negative or ruinous consequences—such as missing out on promotions and advancements, being fired from their jobs, losing their life savings, betraying their families, surrendering their lifelong dreams, and going to prison. A leader must know how to establish a solid foundation for living that will sustain him and keep him on the right path in times of uncertainty, temptation, and crisis.

"Convicted" for Good Character

The judge's comments about Bernie Madoff's character lead us to ask ourselves some probing questions about our own lives:

+ If my family, friends, and colleagues were asked to give a statement under oath in court about the strength of my character, what would they say? Would they be able to talk about my good values and the positive contributions I have made to society?

+ Changing the analogy around, would their testimony be strong enough to "convict" me for my good character? If so, would their assessment be true in light of what I know about myself?

+ How much importance have I placed on having a good name—and the character to back it up?

+ What difference would it make to my family, my business, or my organization for me to be acknowledged as a person of genuine integrity?

✦ Am I living ethically in all areas of my life—such as the ways I work with others, meet my responsibilities, and treat others in the world?

Your Personal Security System

Good character is like a personal security system for your life. Many people install security devices in their homes and places of business to protect them from outside forces—such as thieves who would steal from them and intruders who would do harm to their family members or employees.

Suppose a would-be thief tried to open a window of a home that was electronically "armed" by the security system. An alarm would sound, exposing the intruder, with the goal of scaring him off, while alerting the security company. Or, what if a trespasser managed to sneak into an office building during working hours and lie low until everyone had left for the day? If the security system has been installed properly, the moment he came out of hiding to steal or ransack, the system would detect his movement and set off a signal, alerting security and/or law enforcement officials to his presence.

Good character, or moral force,
is like a personal security system for your life.

We can "install" character in our lives so that it will work like those security systems. We do this by developing values and establishing a code of ethics that will alert us to, and protect us from, the negative effects of various outside influences—such as life's pressures, difficulties, and temptations. These negative influences can threaten our leadership by invading our lives and stealing our willpower, common sense, and better judgment. Values and ethics also safeguard us from internal "intruders"—our own human frailties that cause us to rationalize immoral behavior and take ethical shortcuts.

True leadership has always been built on strong character. That is why we need a new respect for this essential leadership quality. Not only that, but we must immediately begin to promote its restoration. Many leaders today are attempting, unsuccessfully, to separate the ethics of their personal lives from the responsibilities of their public lives. That approach might seem legitimate on face value. Yet below the surface is this crucial reality: Leadership is not just a role one plays; it is a life one leads.

A Foundation of Character

Some people have a cavalier attitude toward ethics and morals—aware of them but essentially disregarding them. However, other people have never really been trained in the principles of character, so they make unwise decisions that lead to their downfall. We can all think of people who were admirable in many ways but fell because they lacked the discretion or discipline that comes from cultivating good character. For example, they may have started associating with "friends" who weren't looking out for their welfare and drew them into illegal activity. Or, they may have begun experimenting with drugs or alcohol because it seemed "fun" or provided a release from life's pressures, only to fall into the snare of addiction.

A failure in character can happen to anyone, in any vocation or stratum of life. For example, there was the case of two elementary school cafeteria workers from Pennsylvania who were described as "sweet, hard working lunch ladies" but who stole more than ninety thousand dollars of lunch money over a period of eight years to feed their gambling addictions.[3] Similar stories have unfolded in communities across the globe.

I recognize that addictions to gambling or to alcohol, drugs, or other substances can be the result of physical predispositions or deep emotional issues. These often require the assistance of a professional counselor. Yet character training is an essential part of the healing process in these cases. As we will see, the development of character in an individual begins with the realization of his value as a human being and an understanding of what he was born to accomplish. With that awareness, he can gain a new sense of self-worth, internal strength, and hope for the future.

No matter what type of leader you are or how widespread your influence, you face personal temptations, challenges, and stresses. And only a foundation of character will sustain you and your leadership.

Leadership is not just a role one plays; it is a life one leads.

"Easier Kept than Recovered"

Thomas Paine wrote, "Character is much easier kept than recovered." Character is like preventive medicine—it keeps you morally healthy so that you won't develop maladies as a result of ethical flaws. One of the most serious of these disorders is untrustworthiness. Once you lose the trust of your family, your friends, or your colleagues, it is very difficult to win it back.

Imagine you owned a business and had been using a particular supplier for many years. Then, the supplier was exposed as having been repeatedly dishonest in his billing practices. Assuming he wasn't put in jail, would you continue to do business with him?

Or, suppose you had supported a particular politician but found out that he had been taking bribes for years, living a lavish lifestyle. Would you continue to support him?

Chances are, no.

We can easily understand why leaders who have ethical defects lose the trust of their followers, because we have all experienced some type of betrayal, as well as the pain and anger it generates. Perhaps you have been overcharged for repair services, had your house broken into and robbed, been blindsided by the unfaithfulness of a spouse, or had a colleague gossip about confidential information you shared. You understand what it means to be a victim of someone who is operating with a character deficit. As leaders, we must ask ourselves, "Am I, in any way, violating the trust of those who have placed their faith in me? What impact am I having on those who are influenced or affected by my behavior?"

Once you lose the trust of others, it is very difficult to win it back.

The Courage to Identify and Root Out Weaknesses

It is not just the Bernie Madoffs of this world who have character flaws. And it is not only "big" ethical issues like fraud and infidelity that erode our integrity, injure our credibility, and wrong others, damaging the quality of our leadership. Character has many practical, everyday implications.

For example, how would you rate your consistency? If you are always delinquent in paying your bills due to carelessness, it can, among other things, affect your credit standing and that of your family or business. One result is that you could miss out on opportunities to acquire loans to expand your company, thereby limiting the growth of your business. In a similar way, if you are regularly late for appointments and meetings, you can erode others' confidence in you and prompt them to decline future collaborations that would have been advantageous for you.

Or, could a lack of self-discipline be undermining your strengths? For instance, do negative emotions such as anger control you? If you hold on to grudges, you may lose out on beneficial relationships, as well as sacrifice your own peace of mind as you waste unnecessary energy dwelling on bitter thoughts. Or, if you allow yourself to abuse alcohol or drugs, you will not only do harm to your health but also put yourself at serious risk of losing the respect of people you value and who can support your leadership (not to mention the ramifications of any legal violations).

All of our negative attitudes and careless behaviors weaken our leadership. The effects of our unaddressed character flaws inevitably cause us damage. Whenever we fail to pay attention to issues of character, we will experience some kind of loss.

The fallen leaders whom we know personally or read about in the headlines are warnings to us. We must recognize that every decision we make adds a sentence to our life story. Will the complete story of your life and leadership add up to something positive and honorable? There is only one way to ensure this outcome—through the intentional development of character.

A leader who desires to be strong and effective will summon the courage to identify and root out his weaknesses.

Most people have certain positive character traits and certain negative character traits. Picture a continuum where some people have moved toward the positive side of character, while some have moved toward the negative side. Where are you on that measure? Are you on the positive side, with conviction and integrity—or on the negative side, with duplicity and moral compromise? Your answer will require some introspection, including an examination of your personal motives. It is easy for us to overlook areas of ethical weakness in our lives, and to remain unaware of how these weaknesses affect the quality of our leadership.

A leader who desires to be strong and effective will summon the courage to identify and root out his weaknesses, preventing them from growing into larger, more damaging issues.

The Priority of Character

There are many components to leadership, but I consider the following three areas to be indispensable: (1) purpose and vision; (2) potential and ability; and (3) values, ethics, and principles. Of these three areas, the most important is the third, because values, ethics, and principles protect a leader's purpose from being sidelined or destroyed.

Purpose and *vision* show a leader what direction he is meant to go in life. All leaders live by a sense of meaning. They believe they are here on earth to do something important for humanity. The knowledge of their purpose is a catalyst, giving them internal motivation.

Potential is a leader's innate gifts and qualities, while *ability* includes all the skills, expertise, education, knowledge, wisdom, and insights a leader has developed and acquired, as well as all the other resources at his disposal that will enable him to accomplish his purpose. Leaders must believe in their own capacity to fulfill the vision that resides in their mind and heart.

Values, ethics, and *principles* relate to a leader's character. They are the standards that a leader establishes for himself—and lives according to—in the process of exercising his potential and ability for the accomplishment of his vision. Consequently, the leader has a sense of responsibility toward himself and others.

> *"The price of greatness is responsibility."*
> —Winston Churchill

Let's shorten the titles of these three components of leadership and simply refer to them as *purpose, potential,* and *principles.* Many leaders do not see principles as being more important than—or even equally as important as—the other two areas. Yet purpose, potential, and principles must all be in balance for leadership to work—they are a trinity of leadership success.

To sum up, leaders need (1) a guiding purpose that generates a passion to accomplish a vision; (2) a recognition of their innate gifts and a commitment to develop them, as well as to gather available resources; and (3) the formulation of values, ethics, and principles that order their conduct and guide the process by which they exercise their leadership. Purpose and potential are never more important than principles, because a lack of principles can nullify them.

The Most Powerful Force

Character is the most powerful force a leader can possess because it protects his life, his leadership, and his legacy—it manifests who he is and shapes who he will become. Without character, every other aspect of leadership is at risk. Let's look at some of the ways that character protects and preserves one's leadership.

Character Protects a Leader's Inner Life

Character establishes a leader's integrity and enables his growth as a person of ethics and values. Leadership training and development must start with the inner life of the leader before it can move on to the principles and process of leadership.

Having character will not prevent you from experiencing various struggles and setbacks in life—all leaders have those. But for long-term personal and professional success—and for the ultimate summation of your life—maintaining character is indispensable.

"Character, in the long run, is the decisive factor in the life of an individual and of nations alike."
—Theodore Roosevelt

Character Extends the Longevity of Leadership

As we have seen, leaders across the globe—in all levels and arenas of society—are being removed from their leadership roles and positions due to ethical violations and moral concerns. Their downfalls have cut short their leadership, causing them to lose their ability to exercise their innate gifts, through which they were meant to fulfill their purpose and vision in life.

A point that we will return to as we explore the nature of character is that leadership is a privilege given by the followers. When a leader violates moral standards, he forfeits the privilege to use his gift in the service of the followers who gave it. Leaders don't have a "right" to be followed. The privilege of leadership is one that leaders must protect through their character and the trust it evokes. Only the power of genuine character can restore the faith in leadership and authority that many people lack today.

I have watched many highly gifted leaders who have manifested a character failure act as if they had done nothing wrong. Believing they could cruise along on their gifts alone, they didn't understand that they had forfeited the opportunity to continue serving their talents and abilities to the world—at least until they had effectively addressed their character defects. Leaders who have fallen need to stop and correct their ethical issues first. Then, they can begin to earn others' trust again, and, hopefully, move forward in genuine leadership.

Businessman Elmer G. Leterman wrote, "Personality can open doors, but only character can keep them open." Your character—not your gift—is the fuel of your leadership. Your gift is validated by your character. So, when your character isn't maintained and starts to "leak," your gift loses the ethical power that propels it.

A leader's gift is only as safe as the character that contains it.

So, while leaders have many opportunities to use their gifts and skills, it is character that ultimately determines the length and effectiveness of their leadership. Years ago, one of my mentors told me, "Whatever you compromise to gain, you will lose." Many people have sacrificed a great future on the altar of compromise. They have taken their potential to impact the world and thrown it away for momentary pleasure or monetary gain.

Jesse Jackson Jr., a former U.S. Congressman and the son of the civil rights leader, was sentenced to 30 months in prison for using campaign funds to make more than 3,000 personal purchases over a period of seven years, totaling approximately $750,000.[4] The prosecutor for the case commented, "Jackson's political potential was unlimited.... He squandered his great capacity for public service through outright theft."[5]

The consequences of lost leadership affect not only individuals but also corporate entities. Energy company Enron went bankrupt and had to sell off all its assets after some of its executives used fraudulent accounting practices to hide its debt. The actions of those executives helped to crack the foundation of the whole company, and their own contributions as leaders were cut short.

Accordingly, leaders must become aware of an often-overlooked, but very real, threat to their leadership longevity: *success.* Don't expect your success to carry you in life. Rather, let your success be carried by your character. Many people cannot handle achievement well because the accompanying responsibility, rewards, and stakes weigh too heavily on them. People can fall into all kinds of moral and ethical problems when they are successful because they suddenly feel all-powerful and unrestrained. They don't realize that they are setting themselves up for a disastrous fall.

People become leaders when they make the decision not to sacrifice their principles on the altar of convenience or compromise.

The great leader Jesus of Nazareth said, "What good will it be for a man if he gains the whole world, yet forfeits his soul? Or what can a man give in exchange for his soul?"[6] In effect, a person can "gain the world" through the power and riches associated with his leadership but, at the same time, forfeit his soul—the very core of his being—by ignoring or betraying his own character. In doing so, he can lose his leadership impact and longevity—not to mention the reason for his very existence. That is a tragic waste of his leadership and his life.

The only way to protect what you hope to accomplish as a leader, and what you have already accomplished, is to develop and maintain strong personal character.

Character Preserves a Leader's Cause and Legacy

As we have noted, a leader's failure can damage the reputation of the government, company, organization, or associates with which he is connected. This truth illustrates another foundational principle that we will explore more fully later on: A leader's values are personal—but they are never private.

Some years ago, when United Way chairman William Aramony was sentenced to prison for embezzling the organization's funds, the news of his actions damaged the charity's reputation. When a scandal occurs within an organization, that organization has to rebuild its reputation and earn the public's trust all over again. The United Way board took immediate action to restore the faith of its donors by hiring as their interim chairman a businessman who was known for his integrity.

A leader's values are personal—but they are never private.

Some leaders fall dramatically and publicly, destroying their legacies in an instant. Other leaders unravel their legacies over a long, slow moral descent that eventually ruins their lives. When the longevity of an individual's leadership is cut short by a character issue, he is often unable to leave the legacy that he was meant to give to his generation. He has to forfeit his vision—or, if not his vision itself, then his own participation in that vision.

Shortly after Lance Armstrong stepped down as chairman of his charity due to doping charges, the charity—which helps those who are dealing with cancer—changed its name from the Lance Armstrong Foundation to the LIVESTRONG Foundation. Former Executive Vice President of Operations Andy Miller said, "We set about charting an independent course forward."[7] Ironically, the name of the charity's founder and former leader had to be removed to help safeguard its future.

No matter how much good a person may have done, his contributions can be overshadowed by even one questionable act. For two hundred years, Elbridge Gerry, a signer of the Declaration of Independence and vice president of the United States, has been more widely remembered for the term that was coined based on his single act of political maneuvering than for any other part of his time in public service: *gerrymandering*.

Hitendra Wadhwa, a professor at Columbia Business School, wrote about one of the characteristics that made Martin Luther King Jr. a great leader and helped to preserve his purpose, message, and legacy. It was his commitment to control his anger at the injustices and insults that were continually hurled against him, and to channel that anger toward constructive purposes. "King had reason enough to be provoked, time and again. He was physically threatened and attacked by bigoted people, repeatedly jailed by state authorities (sometimes on trivial traffic violations), harassed by the FBI and even vilified by fellow black leaders who preferred more aggressive forms of resistance."

Wadhwa then quoted from King's autobiography, in which the civil rights leader recorded how he admonished himself, "You must not harbor anger....You must be willing to suffer the anger of the opponent, and yet not return anger. You must not become bitter." The professor concluded: "Only by taming his own anger did King earn the right to become a messenger of peaceful struggle to the people of the nation."[8]

When we intentionally develop our character, we strengthen our frailties, tame our vices, and prepare ourselves to fulfill our personal leadership role.

Character Prevents a Leader from Hurting Those Around Him

A leader's fall can deeply hurt those close to him and others who have put their trust in him. It can destroy not only his life but also the lives of his victims, the families of his victims, his own family members, his associates, and his associates' families. Returning to the example of Bernie Madoff, the businessman's investors were afflicted with shock, anger, and economic devastation due to his Ponzi scam, as many of them lost much or all of their life savings.

Moreover, not one member of Madoff's family was present in the courtroom to support him when he was sentenced to the longest prison term for fraud ever given.[9] Either he had alienated them by his deception, or they were afraid to be seen with him.

In addition, tragedy has stricken the former tycoon's family. His older son, Mark, committed suicide on the two-year anniversary of his father's arrest.[10] His younger son, Andrew, is currently fighting stage IV cancer of the blood. He had been in remission from the disease, but he feels that "the stress and shame that he dealt with after hearing about his father's... Ponzi scheme caused his cancer to surface again." He declared, "Even on my deathbed I will never forgive him for what he did."[11] Once more, our personal behavior often has consequences for others. We can jeopardize their futures, as well as our own.

The only way to stay focused on your vision and keep moving forward in the midst of the inevitable stress, criticism, attacks, temptations, and setbacks that come with leadership is to develop personal character. The only way to contribute meaningfully to your generation is to maintain character.

What do want to achieve? What do you want to contribute to the world? Character will pave the way to its fulfillment and also protect it.

No Substitute

We are living in difficult social and economic times when we must re-focus on the priority of character—because character is the foundation for all aspects of effective leadership.

Authority, gifts, skill, knowledge, experience, expertise, and so forth are integral elements of leadership, but they can never substitute for char-acter. Unless we want to see the conditions of our world grow increasingly worse, and unless we disregard the lives and legacies of our leaders—and that includes us—we can't move into the future with the same methods and values of leadership that we're employing today. The public has been learning bad habits from its leaders. We must have a course correction—and it must start with each one of us.

Character is the foundation for all aspects of effective leadership.

We face a great "war" today: the struggle between character and compromise. I believe character will ultimately win, as more and more leaders commit to becoming ethically conscious and principled, because true character rests on a strong foundation that has the power to defeat compromise.

All leaders should be encouraged to value integrity so that they will not turn away from their ethical standards and thereby sacrifice the great potential they possess. Those in high office and in other visible positions must take this truth especially to heart. Engineers know that the taller the building, the deeper the foundation must be. Similarly, the more exposure a leader has to the public—the more fame he acquires, the more influence he exerts—the more vigilant he must be to maintain deep, well-established character.

Your Leadership Rests on Your Character

Despite current trends, it *is* possible for leaders to have character in the twenty-first century. We have many examples of people from former times who faced similar challenges with conviction and who can inspire and encourage us. Think of Abraham Lincoln, Mahatma Gandhi, Mother Teresa, and Rosa Parks. Rosa Parks became a leader simply by insisting on being treated equally when she rode the city bus. She refused to sacrifice her principles on the altar of convenience or compromise.

No matter in what domain you are a leader—financial, political, educational, religious, medical, corporate, scientific, artistic, and so forth—your leadership rests on your character. In *The Power of Character in Leadership*, we will explore…

+   What character, or moral force, is, and how to develop it.

+ How your beliefs shape your values, morals, ethics, and principles.

+ How to build your leadership so that it is both effective *and* enduring.

+ How to develop specific qualities of principled leaders.

+ How to be restored after a failure in character.

You will be challenged to assess the strength of your current beliefs and values, and to make a new or renewed personal commitment to ethical leadership. This will necessitate making changes in your life. Yet change is the best thing that can happen to us when we take what is weak and make it strong, and when we take something good and make it even better.

Character matters to you because...

1. It establishes and strengthens your inner life, so that you are a person of integrity and honor.

2. It enables you to effectively fulfill your purpose and potential.

3. It protects your leadership and your vision—preventing you from canceling them prematurely, and enabling you to leave a legacy for your own generation and future generations.

Character matters to the world because...

1. It is the key to inspirational leadership. People need the encouragement and influence of genuine leaders if they are to fulfill their own purposes and live peaceful, productive lives.

2. It safeguards the well-being of those who are under the authority of leaders or are otherwise affected by leaders' actions and influence.

3. It enables leaders to build and maintain healthy communities while addressing critical problems with ethics and integrity.

Your family, community, and nation need you to be a leader of principle. Guard your character, prizing it as "better than silver or gold." Learn the theories and practical skills of leadership, but first establish values and ethics that will free you from moral hindrances and empower you to carry out your singular purpose in life.

2

Leaders of Conviction

"Leadership development is self-development."
—John G. Agno, corporate executive and author

Several years ago, I was sitting at the airport, looking out the window as I watched the arrival of an aircraft that was taxiing down the runway toward my gate. This was the plane that would take me to Nigeria, where I was scheduled to speak at a conference. Suddenly, a seagull flew in front of the window and landed on the ground near where the aircraft would come to a stop.

So, there I was, looking at two "birds." The first one did not have an innate ability to fly—it had been constructed with the mechanical ability to become airborne. But the second one had an inherent physical capacity to fly.

As the plane approached, a number of airline employees started quickly moving around on the nearby tarmac. Two of the workers guided the plane to the jet bridge using green and red lights as signals. Others then positioned the wheel chocks, worked the ramp, plugged in the external power and air, refueled the plane, checked for mechanical issues, and unloaded and loaded the conveyer belts with luggage.

Within the aircraft and behind the scenes, there were a number of others who were involved in flying and maintaining the plane and seeing to the needs of the passengers: air traffic controllers, pilots, flight dispatchers, load planners, flight attendants, and maintenance coordinators, as well as employees who restocked the water and food, serviced the bathrooms, and cleaned out the cabin. I have learned that for a domestic flight, it takes about fifty minutes to "turn" an airplane, preparing it for the next departure. International flights can require an hour and a half. The well-choreographed efforts of many individuals are required to handle the needs of just one jet.

Yet, as I observed the action on the tarmac, I noted that no one ran to help the seagull! The bird didn't need any outside support to keep it running smoothly and safely, and to prepare it to fly again. Flying came naturally to it. Soon, I saw the bird take off from the spot where it had been standing—without jet fuel to propel it, a pilot to guide it, or a long runway to help it get up to speed. It just flew up into the air…and soared.

Leadership Is Inherent

Leadership is designed to function like the flight of a natural bird rather than that of a mechanical plane. That doesn't mean that leaders act independently from others. Quite the opposite. But, as I wrote in chapter 1, leadership is not a role one plays; it is a life one leads. Genuine leadership can never be separated from the essence of the leader as a person. In this way, an individual's exercise of leadership is, in effect, "self-manifestation."

True leaders begin to "fly" when they start living in line with their intrinsic purpose. They don't need artificial props. A leader may have a title, status, and so forth, but he doesn't require those external supports—and they are not what define him as a leader.

Genuine leadership cannot be separated from the essence of the leader as a person.

If you have not yet discovered your inherent leadership purpose, you may have an important position in your company and an impressive job description, but you are functioning only "mechanically" instead of naturally. You are going through the motions, but you are not leading according to the capacity that you were meant to, and you are not experiencing the level of fulfillment that comes with it.

The Vital Connection Between Purpose and Character

Only when a leader discovers who he was born to be, and how his intrinsic gifts determine his personal leadership, can he effectively develop the values, principles, and ethics that lead to strong character. Character is much more than mere rules and regulations for behavior. If we don't understand the relationship between leadership and purpose, the development of our character can be interrupted or blocked. We may always struggle with certain ethical flaws, because we will be functioning according to an "unnatural" basis.

In the next few chapters, we will discover the extent to which the power of character in leadership is tied to personal purpose. Let's begin by investigating how leaders develop.

How Leaders Are Formed

I have trained thousands of leaders in seminars, conferences, and training institutes across the globe. During more than three decades of research, experience, and teaching on leadership, I have read scores of leadership books. From them I've collected hundreds of definitions of leadership. Yet I have never been able to find one definition that incorporates all of the essential ingredients of character-based leadership.

Some years ago, while I was searching for a comprehensive description of leadership, I developed the following working definition. I still find it to be the most useful for helping people grasp the nature of true leaders and for training them in leadership so that they, in turn, can train others.

Leadership is the capacity to influence others through inspiration motivated by a passion, generated by a vision, produced by a conviction, ignited by a purpose.

To understand the process by which an individual becomes a true leader—enabling him to lay a strong foundation for his character—let's reverse the order of the concepts from the above definition in the following sequence:

Purpose

—

Conviction

—

Vision

—

Passion

—

Inspiration

—

Influence

—

Leadership

The process occurs in this way:

+ An individual discovers his purpose.

+ As a result of this discovery, he develops a conviction about what he should be doing with his life, as well as convictions, or foundational beliefs, about how he should live it.

+ His convictions prompt him to conceptualize a clear vision of a preferred future that will enable him to pursue his purpose in a practical way.

+ This vision gives him the passion to carry out his purpose.

+ His passion inspires others to embrace his vision.

+ As others are inspired, they are influenced to take action to help him fulfill his vision.

The evidence of a leader's positive influence on others is the manifestation of his leadership.

Let's look at each of these stages more closely. As we do, I encourage you to evaluate the basis on which you have built your leadership and how you exercise it. What is its foundation? What is its meaning? What energizes it?

1. Purpose

Leadership is not exercised simply by implementing techniques or methods, by using one's skills, or by exhibiting a particular management style. It is the expression of a mind-set resulting from the knowledge of who you were born to be.

We live our lives based on who we think we are and why we think we exist. Therefore, our leadership development to this point has been influenced by our sense of the significance of life and our relationship to it.

Discovering Your Inherent Purpose

A true leader recognizes that he has a special purpose for being in the world. That purpose determines the area of leadership in which he is to serve. His recognition of his particular purpose is not an indication of undue pride. Rather, it is a realistic assessment of his gifts and strengths.

Every person on earth is meant to exercise leadership in a particular area of gifting. One of the ways we discover our purpose is by recognizing the gift we can contribute to the world and/or the problem we were born to solve. This process involves asking ourselves questions such as these:

+ What are my talents?

+ What would I like to do with my life?

+ What do I most enjoy doing?

+ What has been my lifelong dream?

+ What idea do I have that refuses to go away or keeps recurring in my mind?

+ What have I always wanted to do but never thought I would be able to?

+ What injustices make me so angry that I must do something to alleviate them?

King Solomon, the wisest and richest man of his day, said, "A man's gift makes room for him."[1] Your unique gift will make room for you in the world, opening doors of opportunity, while drawing the help and resources you need to fulfill your purpose.

Every person on earth is meant to exercise leadership in a particular area of gifting.

Internally Motivated

Perhaps you have been using your gift to some extent but haven't really applied it with a sense of personal purpose. Or, maybe you have you have been burying your dream, settling for a lesser existence. You may already be very accomplished in a certain field but secretly wish you were doing something different with your life.

If you pursue your true purpose, you will be internally motivated to exercise your inherent gift. In contrast, if you do something you were not born to do, you will have to make an effort to perform it. Maintaining your leadership position or your job will become a burden and a drain on you.

When someone is in the wrong place, he sometimes has to prop himself up with a surplus of support people and resources. But when he finds the place for which he was born, his life begins to flow naturally. He no longer needs to manufacture motivation, because he can't wait to start each day and initiate the next step that will bring him closer to seeing his purpose fulfilled. He's found what he has been looking for in life. He's not even motivated by a paycheck, because a true leader has a need to fulfill his purpose, whether or not he receives compensation. Even so, he discovers that provision comes when he focuses on serving his gift to the world.

If you hate Monday mornings, if you can't wait for the weekend to come, then you are a "jet." But if, after a weekend, you are eager to get back to your work (your corporation, artistic endeavors, volunteer activities, and so forth), you are a "bird"—and not just any bird but an eagle.

Avoiding Ethical Pitfalls

It can be much more difficult to exercise character in leadership if you are in the wrong field, place, or position in life. This is because if you have become frustrated and uncertain in your leadership, you may say and do things that are not honest or forthright, for the purpose of protecting your position or keeping your insecurities from being exposed. If you are motivated not by your inherent purpose but by other impulses—a desire for fame, money, and the like—you will want to do whatever it takes to achieve those ends, and character will take a backseat.

In an address to aspiring lawyers, Abraham Lincoln wrote some wise advice, which we can apply to any field of endeavor:

> There is a vague popular belief that lawyers are necessarily dishonest....Let no young man, choosing the law for a calling, for a moment yield to this popular belief. Resolve to be honest at all events; and if, in your own judgment, you cannot be an honest lawyer, resolve to be honest without being a lawyer. Choose some other occupation, rather than one in the choosing of which you do, in advance, consent to be a knave.[2]

The same principle applies to any arena of endeavor. If you know you cannot have good character while pursuing a certain goal or working in a certain field, then you should cease pursuing that goal or vocation and find your true purpose. You should pursue something that you can do with honesty and integrity. Even when we are functioning according to our purpose, we still have to build and maintain our character, but we can avoid some of the ethical pitfalls that spring from wrong motivations, boredom or apathy, and the fear that others will learn our weaknesses.

When we are functioning according to our purpose, we can avoid ethical pitfalls.

When you are settled into your purpose, insecurities will begin to melt away. You won't wear yourself out trying to please other people; you won't need others constantly telling you that they approve of you and what you are doing. You will like yourself because you will experience your own inner approval as you fulfill what you were born to do. You will also be freer in opening up to other people as you work together to fulfill mutual purposes.

The primary focus of your leadership, therefore, should not be to lead people—that result will develop naturally. Rather, it should be to discern your true self and to pursue your purpose. By exercising your unique gift, you will discover your personal leadership and find meaning, fulfillment, and contentment in your work. And the character it takes to sustain your gift and your leadership is what this book is all about.

You were meant to accomplish something that no one else can accomplish. You were born to do something that the world will not be able to ignore. So, diligently seek your gifts, purpose, identity, potential, and destiny.[3]

2. Conviction

Once a leader discovers his personal gifting and leadership, it ignites conviction in his heart. In the process of leadership development, *conviction* has a twofold connotation. The first sense of the word is a belief in one's significance. This is not just head knowledge. It is the *certainty* that you have something essential to contribute to humanity. It is a 100-percent dedication to your purpose, which is stronger than any opposition you might encounter. As a leader, you must be convinced that you exist for a worthy reason and that you are able to accomplish what you were born to do.

The second sense of the word refers to convictions (plural), or deep-held beliefs based on a commitment to one's purpose. Convictions give you a sense of direction in life. They guide your activities and give them meaning. Your convictions are instrumental to your character development. They lead you to become dedicated to specific principles, or a code of ethics, by which you pledge to live as you carry out your purpose.

An individual can have the other qualities listed in the above definition of leadership, such as influence or passion, without having conviction. But true leaders manifest each of the qualities—and the ingredient we are sorely missing among leaders today is personal convictions. Having convictions is what enables a person to remain stable and trustworthy, even in the midst of difficulties or temptations.

Frankly, if you don't have solid convictions, you don't deserve to have followers. If you keep vacillating in order to please people, if you keep sacrificing your belief system in order to be accepted, you are not a leader—you are a compromiser. We need leaders who are willing to stand up to the disapproval of their own friends and the public at large for the sake of something that is noble and true. Today, it is hard to find leaders who have such commitment to their convictions.

If you sacrifice your belief system in order to please others, you are not a leader—you are a compromiser.

3. Vision

A leader's conviction about his significance propels him to develop a personal vision, as he begins to formulate the specific way in which he will carry out his contribution to his generation. I define vision as "purpose in pictures" or "the future in pictures." It is seeing your purpose so clearly in your mind's eye that it is already a reality to you. All true leaders have a clear vision. They can "see" the objective they hope to accomplish or the product they want to produce.

When Martin Luther King Jr. gave his famous "I Have a Dream" speech, he declared, "I have a dream that my four little children will one day live in a nation where they will not be judged by the color of their skin but by the content of their character."[4] From the clear way he articulated his vision, many of the 250,000 people who heard him speak from the Lincoln Memorial in Washington, D.C., that day—as well as the multitudes who have since heard or read his words—must have virtually seen the future he envisioned.

Vision influences your entire life, including your priorities—how you use your time, what you spend your money on, what opportunities you act upon, and so forth.

What is your personal vision? When you start "seeing" your dream and realizing how your gift can be served to the world, you begin to formulate a vision for your life. And it is through your vision that you will be able to begin the practical process of fulfilling your life's purpose.

4. Passion

Most people have an interest in their future, but they lack the drive to fulfill what they truly desire to accomplish in life. Yet, those who have discovered their purpose, formulated deep convictions, and captured their vision in their mind's eye will have natural enthusiasm and energy. Hard work and diligence are always involved in carrying out one's purpose, but they can be difficult to maintain without internal motivation. Passion provides that motivation.

It is his sense of significance that a helps a true leader to protect his passion from degenerating into mere hunger for power. Tragically, there are leaders in our world who seem to have no trouble killing or otherwise eliminating their opponents and others who are "in their way"—including many innocent people—in order to achieve their ends. But they are not willing to die for something noble. In contrast, the passion associated with true leadership comes from a personal commitment to sacrifice oneself to fulfill one's purpose—even to the point that one would be willing to die for it.

Leadership passion is therefore a desire that is stronger than death. We see evidence of this quality in the lives of great leaders. Abraham Lincoln spoke about his unequivocal commitment to the principle of freedom for all men that is embodied in the Declaration of Independence, asserting, "I have said nothing but what I am willing to live by and, if it be the pleasure of the Almighty God, die by."[5] Nelson Mandela said, "I have cherished the ideal of a democratic and free society in which all persons live together in harmony and with equal opportunities. It is an ideal which I hope to live for and to achieve. But if needs be, it is an ideal for which I am prepared to die."[6]

Mahatma Gandhi was only five foot four inches and had a slight build, but he won a remarkable political victory over the British Empire, freeing

India from colonial rule. He had a vision of equality and justice in India and a conviction about nonviolent protest. He went to jail and was willing to die for this vision. His passion stirred up hundreds of millions of people and brought about sweeping change. That's the power of passion in leadership.

5. Inspiration

In the process of leadership development, inspiration is the point where the leader connects with other individuals; it is where his purpose intersects with their purposes. A leader's passion for his purpose is like a flame, igniting new possibilities in the minds and hearts of other people, causing them to think in new ways and stirring up and revealing the convictions and visions within them. In this way, a leader's vision gives meaning to others' lives as it invites corporate commitment to a noble cause. People's personal vision will always be found within a larger corporate vision.

A leader's passion for his purpose ignites new possibilities in the minds and hearts of other people.

Awakening Others' Sense of Purpose

When you inspire people by your passion for your purpose, you won't need to recruit them to help you, obtain their "vote of confidence," or wait for them to approve you. As you awaken their sense of purpose, they will voluntarily join you in order to fulfill their own contribution to the world through participating in your vision. They will offer their time, energy, resources, and creative power to be part of a larger purpose to which their vision is connected. Likewise, other leaders will inspire different people who will join them, based on their innate purposes and gifting. There is a place for everyone to manifest his personal leadership abilities.

Keep in mind that although true leaders draw other people to their vision, they do not "clone" them to be just like themselves; they do not seek to recreate themselves in others. Rather, they enable others to use their unique gifts and abilities to fulfill their own inherent purposes. It should be clear that people don't receive their personal visions from the leader to whom they are connected—they are enabled to fulfill their own vision as they help the leader enact his.

For example, suppose a leader's vision is to manufacture a safety feature that would help prevent plane crashes under severe weather conditions. He has the idea and enough knowledge of engineering that he believes the device can be developed. However, he can't design and produce it by himself. As he begins to share his vision and passion for this safety feature, he will draw others to him whose personal vision is to participate in airline design and who have the innate gifts to develop and produce such a device.

Free of Manipulation

Just as true leaders don't seek to clone themselves in their followers, they don't try to "collect" followers and supporters in order to make themselves feel good. They may identify particular people they would like to mentor, and invite them to help carry on the overall vision after they are gone, but they never actively try to recruit admirers.

Likewise, a leader who is motivated by his purpose, convictions, vision, and passion never uses or abuses other people. Genuine leaders seek to facilitate the personal visions of their colleagues, executive team members, managers, employees, and family members. At the same time, the manner in which they live out their vision and code of ethics is a positive example to those around them.

Inspiration is the opposite of intimidation and is absent of manipulation. When leaders fail to inspire others, they often resort to manipulation to force people to participate in their plans and do what they want them to do. I've studied many individuals who have portrayed themselves to the public as leaders but who are really professional manipulators. They play on people's fears, use a carrot-and-stick approach, and threaten and coerce them. That is not leadership—that is sophisticated dictatorship.

Every leader must recognize the danger of falling into manipulation. Every day, all over the world, people manipulate their spouses, their children, their friends, their colleagues, their coworkers, their employees, their clients, or their constituents because they do not understand—or respect—the leadership quality of inspiration. The moment you stop in-spiring people and start manipulating them, you cease to be a true leader.

Inspiration is the opposite of intimidation
and is absent of manipulation.

6. Influence

To a large extent, leadership is influence, and all of us already exercise some influence—whether positive or negative. If somebody else is watch-ing you, you are a leader. The moment you have a child of your own to raise, you are a leader. When you know more about a particular subject than others and can teach it to them, you are a leader. When you are placed in a position of responsibility over your peers, you are a leader.

Leaders who exercise positive influence don't try to prove themselves to others. They are more concerned with "manifesting" themselves, or reveal-ing the purpose they were born to fulfill. When you inspire other people through your passion, you never have to announce that you are a "leader." People will think of you as a leader, and will call you one themselves, be-cause you will have motivated them to do something—change the status quo, create something new, find a solution to a problem, and so forth.

The essence of influence is the ability to motivate other people to take action and effect change. You can't lead if you don't influence. You can't influence if you don't inspire. You can't inspire if you don't have passion. And you won't have passion unless you are convinced about your purpose, convictions, and vision.

As I wrote in the introduction to this book, nothing is altered or trans-formed without leadership. As leaders go, so goes the world. Therefore, if we don't do something about the global crisis in leadership we are experi-encing today, the state of our societies is going to grow worse and worse. Moral leadership is urgent in human affairs because the character of lead-ers—for good or for ill—affects the lives of their followers. Let us look at some specific ways in which this influence occurs.

1. Leaders Influence the Mind-set of the Followers

Leaders can transform people's outlook to the point where their perspective becomes completely different from the way they formerly thought. Such influence is a tremendous power that all leaders need to acknowledge and discipline in their own lives, ensuring that they do not abuse it—especially since a change in mind-set almost always leads to a change in behavior.

A leader can use rhetorical skills to convince people that what they believed was good is evil, and vice versa—altering their values and conduct. In Shakespeare's play *Julius Caesar*, after Brutus and his fellow conspirators kill Caesar, believing him to be a tyrant, the character of Mark Antony uses his communication skills to turn the crowd from an admiration for Brutus to a seething desire to kill him and his accomplices. Followers must always weigh the consequences of what they hear and receive from their leaders.

In contrast, an enlightened perspective is a gift that true leaders can give their followers. For example, when Harriet Beecher Stowe wrote the novel *Uncle Tom's Cabin*, she changed the mind-set of tens of thousands of people who had been either neutral toward the institution of slavery or accepting of it. By putting a personal face on the issue, she showed that slaves were people rather than "property," so that many citizens began to support efforts to abolish slavery.

*An enlightened perspective is a gift that
true leaders can give their followers.*

2. Leaders Influence the Characteristics and Attitudes of the Followers

A leader who holds deep convictions can transfer those convictions to others. For instance, he can rouse the fearful so that they will take bold and necessary action in the midst of a crisis. Winston Churchill, through his powerful speeches, stirred the English people to continue standing against Nazi Germany after the fall of France. In one of these speeches, he famously declared, "...the Battle of France is over. I expect that the Battle of Britain is about to begin....Let us therefore brace ourselves to our duties, and so bear ourselves that, if the British Empire and its Commonwealth last for a thousand years, men will still say, 'This was their finest hour.'"[7]

In contrast, a leader who lacks conviction can transfer his complacency or timidity to his followers. There is an account in one of the books of Moses in which Moses sent twelve leaders to scope out the Promised Land before the nation of Israel entered it. When the leaders returned, ten of them expressed their fear of the inhabitants, declaring that they were too strong to defeat: "We seemed like grasshoppers in our own eyes, and we looked the same to them."[8] Two of the leaders insisted they would still be victorious, but the people grumbled and took on the perspective of the ten who were afraid and felt like "grasshoppers" in their own eyes. As a result, the victory was delayed for forty years—almost two generations. The people lost out, largely because they allowed the fearful mind-set of their leaders to infect them.

3. Leaders Influence the Morality of the Followers

The ethics of a leader can sway those who follow him—either directly, through the corporate values that are encouraged through his leadership, or through his policies. If the leader is a high-ranking official over a nation, his morals can permeate an entire culture. You may come from a country in which the leaders have tremendous gifts, communicate well, and are competent in various leadership techniques—but are lacking in ethical convictions. Many leaders do not take responsibility for their actions. They feel they should experience no consequences when they betray the trust of their constituents, whether their employees, their families, or the public.

Such attitudes and behaviors do not go unnoticed by followers, so that many people begin to think, *He's a leader, and he did such and such and got away with it, so I can do it, too.* This is why it is vital for leaders to recognize and assess the values they currently hold and to establish or reestablish ethical principles that they will commit to stand upon. We will explore this process in the next few chapters.

4. Leaders Influence the Commitment of the Followers

If a leader has strong convictions, his passion will become contagious among his followers, leading them to commit to his vision. Earlier, we talked about Martin Luther King Jr. in relation to how leaders develop vision. King's vision gave him a passion that inspired and influenced "average" people—such as housewives, carpenters, masons, teachers, and religious leaders—to march in nonviolent protest against the refusal of certain states in the nation to acknowledge and permit voting rights for blacks. A number of them personally faced the resistance of policemen armed with clubs, dogs, water hoses, and tear gas. Why would anyone willingly risk being beaten with a billy club or choked by tear gas? What kind of man would influence people to actually do that? Someone with genuine conviction.

A leader's commitment can be transferred to enough people that his personal conviction eventually becomes a national movement. His principles can initiate an irresistible process of reform. If, as a leader, you try to avoid an issue or a consequence, people won't follow you. But if you meet it squarely and remain constant in your convictions, others will join you.

A leader's principles can initiate an irresistible process of reform.

5. Leaders Influence the Destiny of the Followers

The influence of someone who has conviction can lead people to a destiny they might not otherwise have reached. Czech playwright and dissident Václav Havel, who had long decried the dehumanizing elements of communism, helped precipitate the nonviolent Velvet Revolution in Czechoslovakia in 1989 that effectively led to the end of communist rule there. Havel and other dissidents formed the Civic Forum to plan the dismantlement of communism in their country. Timothy Garton Ash, a historian who witnessed the forum, said, "It was extraordinary the degree to which everything ultimately revolved around this one man....In almost all the forum's major decisions and statements, he was the final arbiter, the one person who could somehow balance the very different tendencies and interests in the movement."[9] Havel became the last president of Czechoslovakia and the first president of a new Czech Republic.

Conversely, the influence of a leader who lacks character can condemn his followers to an appalling fate. In the 1970s, cult leader Jim Jones convinced people to leave loved ones and live with him in the jungles of Guyana. Several years later, he led 909 of his followers to their deaths by inducing them to drink cyanide—then he shot himself to death.

Adolf Hitler was a gifted politician and communicator, wielding tremendous influence over the German people. He held thousands of citizens spellbound as they listened to his speeches in person or on the radio. His oration was so powerful that some people thought he was a god. Hitler had many characteristics of an effective leader. But his philosophy, his personal code of ethics, was immoral. It turned his leadership assets into frightening tools of abuse.

Hitler didn't value all of human life—just a small segment of it. His warped value system created disaster for his nation and many other nations of the world. Millions of people died as a direct or indirect result of his reign. They were starved, died of disease, or were exterminated in concentration camps, prison camps, and quarantined ghettos. While fighting World War II—a war Hitler instigated—many people were killed in battle or died when they succumbed to disease or accident; others were wounded, maimed, or emotionally scarred for life. Multitudes lost loved ones and possessions, seeing their entire way of life vanish. Today, the German people are still trying to come to grips with the question, "How could our people have let that happen and even have participated in it?"

The lesson for us is that whatever we accommodate, we will either ultimately embrace or be destroyed by. We are not safe on any level—social, economic, emotional, physical, or spiritual—if we don't know the person we are following. We can't afford to be complacent or gullible.

Study and Evaluate Your Leaders

Our culture teaches us to be impressed by a leader's power, oratorical skills, academic degrees, and/or wealth, thinking that those characteristics add up to great leadership. Yet you must not imagine that your country will remain strong and established if you vote for someone just because you like the way he speaks or looks, or even if you approve of some of his accomplishments.

Before you follow anyone, you must know what that person truly believes and on what path he is taking you. You might find out too late that you don't want to go where he is going. I encourage you not to place undue confidence on how powerful a leader is or how much knowledge he has or who his mentor was. Continually evaluate what your leaders stand for, as well as the policies they promote. Study their lives and convictions. Discover what they really think and value, and how their beliefs affect their policies.

Ask yourself questions such as these about individual leaders:

+ Does he still have the same convictions that inspired me to follow him in the beginning?

+ Does he share my beliefs and values?

+ Does he demonstrate that he has ethical standards?

+ What is his vision of life?

+ What is his attitude toward other human beings?

+ What does he see as the future of this company/organization/community/nation?

+ What direction does he think the world should be taking?

Even if a leader's beliefs seem good, you must still observe his life to see if his words and actions are consistent—if he lives according to his stated convictions.

"If the Blind Lead the Blind..."

I consider Jesus of Nazareth to be the greatest leader in history, and He warned, "If a blind man leads a blind man, both will fall into a pit."[10] Note that the blind leader doesn't fall into the pit by himself. Both he and the blind man whom he is leading fall into it together. We have to make sure our eyes are fully open, so that we will know where our leaders are taking us, and can avert potential disaster. We must not allow ourselves to fall into a pit with them.

Moreover, since we are all leaders or aspiring leaders in our unique areas of gifting, we have a responsibility to those whose lives we influence.

That is why it is essential for us to understand the priority of character before we move on to the other aspects of leadership. We might understand many of the keys and principles necessary for being a leader but, at the same time, embrace a negative or destructive philosophy that will undermine our leadership and hurt our followers.

Leadership influence is a powerful instrument, and we must always be aware of its potential to bring either good or harm to others. Leaders without character demonstrate power devoid of principles; they often manipulate people to achieve their own ends. But true leaders have a commitment to ethics and principles; they build up others and offer them a better life. *

The Distinguishing Marks of a True Leader

People are looking for leaders who have the qualities on the list we have been discussing. In the progression of leadership development, the stage in which one develops conviction is key for leaders if they are to move from the recognition of their purpose to establishing a solid foundation for becoming a genuine leader. It is not enough to know that you have a special gift that will give you a unique place in the world. You must be able to serve that gift in accordance with ethical principles that you are committed to follow as you pursue your vision.

Conviction and character are therefore the distinguishing marks of a true leader. They are what separate those who merely have titles, positions, and talents from those who make a positive difference in their families, communities, and nations—from those who make history, changing the course of human events for the better.

Consequently, the twenty-first-century leader must not seek only to find his purpose or to develop his vision. He must also desire to be introduced—or reintroduced—to ethical principles, and he must commit to developing character throughout his lifetime, demonstrating his trustworthiness to those who follow him.

Our attitudes and motivations always correspond to our character. In part III of this book, we will look at how to develop specific character qualities of true leaders. For now, let us keep in mind the following points:

+ Leadership, and the gifts that enable it, are inherent endowments.

+ Leadership is not about gaining followers—it is about pursuing purpose.

+ Leadership is not about manipulating people—it is about inspiring people.

+ Leadership is not about having power over people—it is about empowering people.

+ Leadership is not about controlling others—it is about serving them.

+ Leadership is not about doing—it is about becoming a person of noble aspirations.

Will you be a leader of conviction? Will you lead the way for others to become leaders of conviction by following your example?

PART II:

The Source of Moral Leadership

3

How Character Develops, Part I:
What We Believe

"We lead out of our beliefs."
—Dr. Myles Munroe

A s I observed the 2012 presidential campaign in America, I noted that the candidates declared, "You have a choice of which America you want." They kept using the word *choice*. Other presidential campaigns have used similar language. The candidates were presenting two different ideas, or philosophies, to the voters. To put it very simply, the choice they were offering was between "big government" and "big business." The personal beliefs of the candidates became the public policy they pursued as leaders.

The same principle is true for all leaders. We lead out of our beliefs.

The Progression of Character Development

All people follow generally the same course as they develop character, whether that character ultimately ends up positive or negative. The process occurs like this:

+ Our beliefs lead to our convictions.

+ Our convictions produce our values (which are tied to our attitudes and perceptions).

+ Our values form our morals, or principles.

+ Our morals/principles lead to corresponding personal conduct. Especially in the case of positive character, morals and principles also prompt us to exercise personal discipline for the purpose of remaining aligned with our convictions.

+ Our conduct/disciplined actions manifest as our ethics.

+ Our ethics result in our character.

+ Our character determines our lifestyle.

In chapter 2, we examined the process by which a person becomes a leader, including the development of convictions based on his purpose. In this chapter, we will look more closely at the manner in which we form our beliefs and convictions. And, for the next three chapters, we will explore traditional perceptions of leaders and leadership, as well as how we can direct the development of our character so that we may become—and remain—ethical leaders.

Philosophy, or Beliefs

Our philosophy, or belief system, has been formulated throughout our lives by our responses to various influences on us. Those influences include our families, our friends, our heritage/background, our physical and social environments, our education, our religious affiliation, our knowledge, the media we have been exposed to, our associates, our coworkers, and so forth. Our beliefs come from the ideas we have been exposed to or have developed from our observations and analyses, and which—and this is most important—we have received as truth.

Some of the ideas we accept may be false or incomplete. But if we believe they are true, they still become incorporated into our personal philosophy, helping to construct the foundation on which we build our lives. That is why, if a person wants to change his belief system, he has to change his ideas about himself and/or his ideas about the world.

We develop character, therefore, as a result of our personal philosophy, including what we believe about the meaning of life, the nature of the world, and how we should relate to other people.

If a person wants to change his belief system, he has to change his
ideas about himself and/or his ideas about the world.

What Ideas Have We Accepted?

I am convinced that one of our greatest weaknesses as leaders today is that our philosophical training about who we are as human beings—including our inherent purpose as leaders—has been severely deficient. Our environment and other influences have produced defects in our thinking due to some of the flawed philosophies that have been perpetuated by our culture, which we have accepted. If we want to become leaders of character who make a positive difference in the world, we need to take a serious look at what ideas we have received, how those ideas have shaped our philosophy of life, and what beliefs and attitudes we may need to change.

For example, if a leader has accepted the concept "It's everyone for himself in this world," he will always put himself before other people, with the result that he may neglect, mistreat, or even abuse his followers. True leaders always place the highest value on the dignity of all humankind. Personally, I believe that if you don't respect other people, you should not be in leadership. The world already has too many problems to take on another leader who disregards the intrinsic value of human beings.

A leader's personal beliefs about himself and the nature of the world will inevitably be revealed in his public policy. By "public policy," I do not refer only to governmental programs and laws. I use the term in a broad sense, to indicate the policies, directives, instructions, and guidance of leaders toward those who follow them. A leader's public policy reflects how he views, interacts with, and affects the lives of other people as he carries out his leadership.

"As a Person Thinks in His Heart, so Is He"

Let us look at another proverb from the perceptive King Solomon: "As [a person] thinks in his heart, so is he."[1] Many people misquote this saying by leaving out the word "heart." But Solomon did not say, "As a person thinks, so is he." To me, the word "heart" is the most important word in this statement. It denotes the center of our reasoning. I believe the "heart" is equivalent to what psychologists today call the "subconscious mind." So, we could paraphrase Solomon's saying in this way: "As a person thinks in his subconscious mind, so is he."

As the term indicates, our subconscious mind exists behind our conscious mental functions. It is where everything that we believe is "stored," much like information is stored on a computer hard drive. When you are using a particular program on your computer, you don't see all the programs and files that exist on your hard drive. You see only what you are working with at the moment, whether it is a word processing system, a spreadsheet, or a game—or several programs at the same time. The rest of the programs and files exist, and some may even be active, but you're not consciously aware of them. Yet if you intentionally open a new file or maximize a screen to view a program you are running (for instance, to check the status of an ongoing system update), you bring that other portion of the hard drive to the attention of your conscious mind, where you can consider it.

In a similar way, we can bring the thoughts that are in our "heart," or subconscious mind, to the surface of our conscious mind for reflection and assessment so that we can begin to evaluate what we really believe—and why.

Most people live according to the ideas that reside in their subconscious mind. That's why it's so important for us to understand not just what another person is saying but what is stored in his belief system. For example, you may have had the experience of thinking that a person had all the makings of a good leader—until he was promoted! Then the negative qualities started to manifest. Abraham Lincoln said, "If you want to test a man's character, give him power." I would augment that apt comment by saying that if you want to know the true character of a person, give him one or all of the following: (1) power, (2) position, or (3) money. The way in which an individual uses any of these resources will reveal what exists at the core of his inner life.

We can sum up what we have discussed so far in this way: Our beliefs govern who we are, as well as the path along which we are traveling in life. It's not what we say, but what we genuinely believe, that directs our lives and our leadership.

Ask yourself, "What foundational beliefs direct my life?"

Convictions

Our established belief system gives rise to our convictions. This point is similar to what we discussed in the last chapter in relation to discovering one's purpose—that when a leader fully believes in his inherent purpose and gifting, it leads to conviction. We can't "receive" character from something outside of us. The groundwork of character is established when we personally hold to an idea so completely that, for us, it becomes a deep principle worth sacrificing for.

Character is measured by the depth of what we claim to believe. Again, you can learn all the skills, methods, and styles of leadership, but they won't mean much if you have no real convictions that guide your life—or if you sell out your convictions. If your belief system is weak, you will find yourself to be inconsistent in your standards and vacillating in your ethics. You may choose the honorable course one day, but the next day engage in ethically questionable behavior.

Ask yourself, "What strong convictions do I hold?"

Character is measured by the depth of what we claim to believe.

Traditional Leadership Concepts: Legacies of Philosophy

Based on the process we have been looking at, we can understand how, through shared beliefs, certain concepts of leadership have taken hold in our nations and permeated the world's cultures. The generally accepted images of leaders and leadership that many people have today are derived from particular philosophical ideas. We have absorbed these ideas as naturally as we have absorbed other ways of thinking and living from our culture, such as the manner in which we celebrate holidays and the colloquialisms we use. Yet most of us haven't stopped to consider how our beliefs about leadership have been affected by prevailing cultural ideas.

The theoretical foundation for many of our beliefs about leadership, especially in Western nations, was derived from the ideas of several renowned philosophers from ancient Greece. These ideas were disseminated widely through the influence of the vast Roman Empire.

The Roman Empire existed for nearly eight hundred years, from about 250 B.C. to A.D. 476. It was the most powerful empire in history. At its height, Rome ruled over virtually the entire known world. No nation or empire since then has equaled its power and influence. The Romans admired the Greeks, and their thinking was greatly influenced by Greek philosophy. The Greeks held the idea that there were superior and inferior races. When Rome invaded Greece and took over that great empire, the Romans adopted this philosophy. They ruled with the idea that Romans were superior to the rest of the peoples of the world. As we will see, the basis of their perceived superiority was that they had certain distinctive traits, and that they had been chosen by the "gods" to be the leaders.

The Romans' philosophy led them to accept the idea that subjugating other peoples was a good and acceptable practice. As their empire extended across the world, their ideas about races and peoples influenced how they treated their subjects and how their subjects came to think about themselves. The essence of these ideas still affects us today.

I have read the writings of Plato and Aristotle, and the thoughts of Socrates. While they said many helpful things, I am astonished that people still accept much of what they believed about leadership, because, in my view, their basic theories are flawed.

Let us examine some of our widely accepted theories of leaders and leadership that come from Greek philosophy.

1. The "Birth Trait" Theory

This theory holds that some humans are born with unique qualities that earmark them for leadership, while the majority of people—who do not possess these traits—are destined only to follow and be subordinate. Aristotle said that from the hour of a person's birth, he was marked for either leadership or subjection. Aristotle promoted the concept that we sometimes express today in these words: "Leaders are born, not made."

I have investigated the traits that the Greeks and Romans valued, and they were things like the shape of one's nose, the color of one's eyes and hair, the fairness of one's skin, and one's height. If you didn't happen to have the preferred manifestations of these traits through genetics, you were automatically relegated to a lesser status—to servitude.

Earlier, we discussed how people often choose leaders based on the leaders' appearance and stature, rather than for their character or even their abilities. Various studies have clearly indicated that personal traits, as well as circumstances, do contribute to the kind of leadership a person exercises. Yet while a person's leadership may be affected by his physical traits and other factors, these do not constitute the whole picture of leadership.

Moreover, some people today have the idea that only individuals with certain traits can be leaders, reinforcing the ancient belief that leaders are superior to the rest of the population. Yet, as we discussed in chapter 2, every person exercises leadership in a particular area of gifting. We all have a unique gift or gifts, and none of us is intrinsically "superior" to others— even when they are under our authority or oversight.

2. The "Chosen by the Gods" Theory

Another Greco-Roman theory that corresponds to the "birth trait" theory is that leadership is reserved for a favored few whom the "gods" selected for elite positions over the masses. The "chosen ones" are to control, manage, and direct the lives, aspirations, fortunes, and futures of those who are "not chosen."

To the people living in the Roman Empire, this meant that if the gods didn't choose you to be a leader, you were destined to spend your life as a slave or a servant. So, if you were not a Roman—a member of the elite race—your lot in life was to be second class. You could never rise to the caliber of someone worthy of real leadership.

This theory supports the idea of a class system. If you believe the gods choose some people to be rulers and others to be slaves, then if you happen to be among the slaves, it wouldn't matter if you earned five PhD's and knew more than all the other leaders combined—you would always be seen as inferior and existing primarily for the benefit of those who were born leaders. In most countries, up until modern times, people did not move from a lower class to a higher one. If they were born to parents who belonged to the nobility or upper class, they remained in that station throughout their lives. If they were born to parents who were servants, they couldn't aspire to be anything but a servant.

We still see this attitude today in many nations among those who think that a person's "pedigree," social status, and education at exclusive schools alone qualify him to be an elite leader. Those whose lineages are from "lesser" origins, and whose social standing and education are not as prestigious, cannot aspire to the highest and most influential leadership roles.

3. The "Charismatic Personality" Theory

This theory promotes the idea that only certain individuals who possess a unique measure of "charisma"—who are extroverted and charming, have superb communication skills, and so forth—are leaders.

Charisma is a Greek word meaning "favor" or "gift." So again, the idea was that certain people were endowed by the gods with gifts that made them superior to others. Today, when they encounter someone who has charisma and charm, many people automatically assume he is a leader or destined to become a leader.

A person with a charismatic personality can use his natural gift while exercising his leadership, but it will not make him a true leader—neither will it sustain him as a leader. Note that each of the above theories has nothing to do with a leader's character, only his personal features or natural abilities. Furthermore, according to these theories and their offshoots, many people today who are active leaders in business, economics, education, religion, science, and many other fields could never have been leaders.

4. The "External Factors" Theory

In addition to the above ideas from the Greeks and Romans, our culture has other traditional views of leadership that focus mainly on external factors. One such view is that leaders are formed as they learn to deal with particular circumstances: If you put a person in a certain situation with specific criteria and stimuli, he will emerge as a leader.

While outside circumstances play a critical role in shaping the character and abilities of leaders (a topic we will explore later), this theory does not generally emphasize a leader's inner purpose, beliefs, and convictions—all of which are essential for successful leadership.

Another idea is that leaders are developed by studying leadership at a college or university, or by participating in other leadership courses and training. Many people believe that if a person has earned an MBA or attended leadership conferences, he is qualified to lead others.

I am not opposed to leadership training—I train leaders all the time. Yet many leadership courses do not cover some of the essential elements of leadership development, such as we discussed in chapter 2. In addition, education and training alone are not sufficient means for becoming a leader—especially if a person does not merge his training with the knowledge of his unique purpose and the exercise of his intrinsic gifts.

A Perpetual Influence

Let us look briefly at how the Greek and Roman ideas of leadership found their way to us. When the Roman Empire eventually fell apart, it became many local states and kingdoms, which developed into the countries we know today. Much of Europe is made up of former colonies of the Roman Empire, and through the influence of various European nations on their own colonies, Greco-Roman philosophies, including those about leadership, spread even farther.

Assumed Superiority

When some of these European nations starting obtaining their colonies, they embraced the idea of the superiority of certain races, in which the oppressor believes he is superior to the oppressed. Over the years, this concept solidified as the idea that a leader is superior to his followers. This damaging philosophy is still taught in a number of our colleges and universities, seminaries, and leadership training schools, which produce many of the leaders of our nations.

This is why, when university graduates and professionals obtain positions of leadership, many of them automatically feel superior to others.

They may not consciously realize they have this attitude; it may exist in their subconscious minds. However, it manifests in their attitudes toward their leadership roles and in their relationships with other people—especially their followers, employees, or subordinates.

Sometimes, the worst thing you can do is give someone a title, because suddenly he thinks, *I am better. I am privileged.* Whether the title is president, executive, senior partner, supervisor, director, manager, pastor, or anything else, it becomes a problem for many people because their minds are still influenced by these false philosophies of leadership.

I find this to be the case among people all over the world. I often speak to groups in developing countries. Of the approximately 7 billion people on earth, about 5 billion of them live in nations that were formerly colonies of European powers. In these nations, the belief system remains that only particular people have the right to lead, and the rest of the masses, who don't have special traits, charisma, and so forth, can never be leaders.

> *Sometimes, the worst thing you can do is give someone a title, because suddenly he thinks,* **I am better. I am privileged.**

The "Black Crab Syndrome"

The sad fact is that those who have been oppressed don't seem to take on a different mind-set once they throw off their oppression and experience a measure of freedom. They suddenly adopt the same philosophy and attitudes toward their own people that had been used against them. For example, they may think, *My skin color is lighter than yours, so I must be better.* Why do people do this? Because it is the model of authority and power they have learned from their culture and by their personal experiences, so that it is ingrained in their thinking and attitudes.

Thus, they act according to the "black crab syndrome," which keeps their emerging societies from becoming places where all people are valued and encouraged to better themselves. The black crab syndrome is a phenomenon named after the behavior of real crabs. Suppose you caught or purchased some live black crabs to serve at a party. You plan to prepare them later on that day, and you need to store them somewhere. You could just place the crabs together in a barrel, and you wouldn't even have to put a lid on top of the container. You could be assured that none would escape. Why? Because the other crabs wouldn't allow a single crab to climb over the rest to reach the opening at the top. If a crab were to climb up so that it got close to the top, the others would pull him back down again. Yet if the crabs would only allow each other to reach the top, many could go free.

This mind-set of not wanting someone else to get ahead of you, and therefore not helping him and even actively working to keep him down—or pulling him down when he begins to succeed—is also prevalent among people in developed nations. Everyone is afraid that someone else will become better off than he is or gain more advantages than he has.

Thus, the leadership mind-sets of the Greeks and Romans still rule us. We think we need to be superior to others in order to feel special, chosen, and safe.

Misfocused Priorities

Due to the above views that we have inherited through our culture, the professors and other instructors who teach leadership courses and seminars at our universities, institutes, and workshops usually focus on such aspects of leadership as these: power, position, titles, skills, gifts, talents, educational qualifications, knowledge, and personality. They do this because these are the ideas that they were taught or otherwise assimilated into their belief systems.

Therefore, in both formal and informal settings of leadership training and practice, we continue to overemphasize certain concepts of leadership while neglecting the most important—character. Again, many of the above ideas are factors in leadership, but they do not define what it means to be a true leader. Most important, they do not *produce* a true leader.

Perhaps 90 percent of the people we consider leaders found their way into their leadership position based on the traditional leadership theories we've discussed. They possess outstanding gifts and skills, they hold impressive academic credentials, they were born into wealthy and/or prestigious families, they exercise some form of natural power and influence, or they have appealing physical traits. While directors, managers, human resources personnel, and electors may have considered the leaders' character when hiring or voting for them, it likely wasn't the first, second, or perhaps third consideration for many of them.

I want to emphasize again that natural attributes and acquired skills have not prevented numerous leaders from failing at their responsibilities and falling from their former heights due to indiscretion, greed, or hubris—thereby destroying their own potential. In the introduction to this book, we looked at a number of famous people who possessed traits that, according to traditional thinking, should have guaranteed their success as leaders, yet they fell. You probably know of other leaders who had all the indications of promising lives and careers but forfeited their positions.

> *"To educate a man in the mind and not in morals*
> *is to educate a menace to society."*
> —Theodore Roosevelt

The Path to Character

What we believe about leaders and leadership has a tremendous effect on what type of leader we become and whether we will fulfill our inherent leadership purpose. It determines whether the path we embark on, guided by our personal beliefs and convictions, will lead us to develop honorable character that will support our leadership or will lead us to develop character flaws that will undermine it.

In the next chapter, we will continue to study the process of character development by looking at the nature and role of values.

4

How Character Develops, Part II: What We Value

"A people who values its privileges above its principles soon loses both."
—Dwight D. Eisenhower, 34th president of the United States

The type of character that is ultimately produced in a person's life is determined by the nature of his beliefs and the focus of his convictions, both of which are expressed in his values.

Many people today are confused about values. In a number of nations, values have been shifting. People aren't sure which values they should continue to hold in high esteem and which they should let go of. Some of the changes in values have been beneficial, while others have been detrimental, contributing to a breakdown of ethical standards in various societies.

Moreover, because many people do not stop to consider what they really believe, and what convictions they hold, they may not be fully aware of what their values are. Instead of establishing their own value system, they act primarily on the viewpoints and sentiments of others, such as family members, friends, coworkers, and celebrities or other opinion makers.

Determining One's Own Values

We all necessarily begin life guided by the views and advice of others. However, as we grow physically, emotionally, mentally, socially, and spiritually, we must make our own decisions about what we believe, what our convictions are, and what we value. If we don't, we will not be able to develop into leaders of character who are guided by internal motivations.

At any stage of our lives, it is a wise practice for us to seek the counsel of two or three people we trust before making a major decision. Yet suppose we receive conflicting advice? If we have no established parameters on which to make a final conclusion or decision, we will never gain a sure footing in life and will continually waver between opinions. Our values and behavior will be based mainly on others' preferences. While it is important to keep an open mind about complex issues, we have to establish a belief system and determine what values we will stand for.

What Are Values?

To help us comprehend the nature of values, let's look at two related definitions. Values are...

+ *Ideas, principles, and qualities on which you personally place high worth.* A value is a belief—in something or someone—that you esteem, on its own merits. For instance, you may value the idea of giving charitable aid to families whose wage earner has been laid off from work, or the principle of "equal justice under law," or the quality of courage.

+ *Standards or ideals that determine your conduct or policy.* To use a simple example, suppose you own a diamond ring, and you know the market value of diamonds and want to protect your asset. The value you place on your diamond ring will both predict and affect your behavior toward it. If you truly value it as a possession, you will keep it clean and put it in a safe place when you're not wearing it. You may even check on it periodically to make sure it has not been lost or stolen.

Properties of Values

Next, let's note several properties connected with values.

1. Values Grow out of Personal or Corporate Philosophy

Again, our beliefs and convictions are always the starting place for the development of our character, which is established through our values.

2. Values Are More Important than Rules

If an individual has strong, positive values, he doesn't require a lot of external laws and rules to govern his life. He doesn't need to be monitored by someone else who makes sure he does what he should be doing. He monitors himself. And because his values are based on his internal motivations, they have both stability and longevity.

The best kind of rules are meant to make us aware of standards that are right and beneficial for us, so that we can make a personal decision to observe them. They are not intended to be an end in themselves. On the other hand, arbitrary rules that people are forced to comply with will lack power because they will not be internalized by them.

If an individual has strong values, he doesn't need a lot of external laws and rules to govern his life.

---

3. Values Can Build Others Up or Tear Them Down

Depending on whether a person's values are derived from positive or negative beliefs, they will be helpful or harmful to the one who holds them—and to others. This point may seem obvious, but many people don't consider the effect their values have on their daily lives.

For example, a leader can value the idea that the financial "bottom line" is the only thing that matters. Accordingly, instead of inspiring his employees, he harasses them in an attempt to attain greater productivity.

The organization Leadership IQ conducted a study involving more than five thousand leaders over the period of August 2012 to January 2013. When asked about their leadership style, 39 percent of the leaders preferred to use an "intimidating" style—a factor the study attributed to "economic fatigue" related to the global financial crisis. Apparently, in an attempt to spur workers to make more money for the company, many managers employed intimidation.[1]

Another study that examined the leadership implications of the economic crisis concluded that leadership based on principles of character was "prevalent in the firms that weathered and even prospered during the crisis."[2] This study indicates how different values can produce different results. Good productivity is a legitimate goal for a leader; however, the path to achieve it is to lead with character, valuing the contributions of each participant and encouraging him to use his gifts to the fullest.

Values ultimately motivate our conduct, and many of our actions are not morally neutral—they have either positive or negative consequences for ourselves and others.

4. Values Are Personal—but They Are Never Private

This point, which I mentioned briefly in chapter 1, corresponds with the previous point. It highlights the fact that our values inevitably have some impact on others.

Many families, communities, and countries are being destroyed today as people's negative values are manifested in their ill treatment of others. For instance, if an individual doesn't place a high value on the institution of marriage—and on his own marriage, in particular—he may think it's acceptable to engage in an extramarital affair. By so doing, he can devastate the lives of his spouse and children. In the process, he may also experience losses—of his friends, his home, and other important aspects of his life.

In contrast, if a person places a high value on the institution of marriage, and has committed himself to this value, it will keep him from having an extramarital affair, even if he may be tempted to do so. His dedication to his marriage will impact not only his life but also the lives of his spouse and children.

5. Values Outlive Goals

Goals are temporary aims that a leader has determined are necessary to enable him to reach a greater objective. Values, on the other hand, are timeless. Once a leader reaches a specific goal in the process of pursuing his vision, he can set other goals that align with his values.

6. Values Send a Message

Your stated values communicate what you claim to stand for. But the values you demonstrate by your actions reveal what you truly stand for and whether your stated values have real substance and meaning.

We should take time to consider what ethical messages we are sending to others. For example, by his words and actions, an individual can indicate to other people that he is open to engaging in unethical behavior. As a result, someone who is looking for a "partner in crime" to participate with him in dishonorable conduct, such as lying or cheating, will feel comfortable in approaching him. However, if the individual has made it clear through his words and actions that he is a person of character who will not lie or cheat, the dishonorable person will not approach him but will pass over him and look for someone else to recruit.

7. Values Attract Similar Values

Likewise, it is generally the case that people who hold particular values are drawn to other people who hold the same values. Applying this point to personal relationships, we know that friendships are forged among people who have similar interests and preferences.

My close friends and associates share my values. There are other people with whom I am unable to associate. My experiences with them have revealed that they don't value the things I value; in fact, sometimes they value things that I believe are detrimental. That doesn't mean that I intentionally snub them. Yet, as a leader, I have to protect my character, and a close tie with them would not only be ethically unhealthy for me but it might also give the impression to others that I support their values.

Values are so important that they should be the basis of our key associations. The same point applies to corporate relationships—for example, companies doing business with one another and governments making agreements and treaties with other countries and supporting various international causes. When considering an association, leaders should ask themselves, "What overt or underlying values are involved in this decision? What binding alliances am I making?"

Global terrorism is on many people's minds today, and terrorists use various methods to promote their causes. When a terrorist straps a bomb to his body and detonates it in a crowded public square, killing innocent people (as well as himself), it indicates that he values his message more than he respects human life. Some people in the world would support his action, because they share a similar priority. Yet the terrorist's demonstration does not lead me to be sympathetic to his cause, and I cannot accept his justification for his actions, because he doesn't respect what I value.

Values should be the basis of our key associations with others.

8. Values Shape Corporate Entities

The social norms and the environment of a corporate entity are established by the values of its leaders and the shared values of its members—creating a corporate culture. In a later chapter, we will discuss the role of core values in relation to a business, an organization, a nation, or any other group.

9. Values Manifest in Corporate or Public Life

A person's values will eventually be revealed by the way he conducts himself, and the manner in which he treats others, in the group of which he is a part. For example, if one of his values is honoring the purposes and inherent gifts of other people, he will not gossip about others or try to undermine their success. If another of his values is respecting the property of others, he will not steal from his company, his coworkers, or his fellow citizens. If yet another of his values is esteeming the quality of honesty, he will not lie to others or exaggerate the facts of a matter to his own advantage.

How Values Function in Our Lives

All true leaders adhere to a value system by which they consider options for conduct, make decisions, and take action. A leader of character is identified by the positive values that he considers worthy, and by which he has determined to live. For positive values to make a difference in your life and leadership, you must progress through the following steps:

1. Identify Your Values

Carefully think through what you truly value and then express your values in writing. Writing down the ideas and behaviors on which you place high worth will help you to identify and clarify them. In addition, if your values are recorded in written form, you can put them in an accessible place (such as a folder in your desk or a file on your laptop), so that you can continually refer to them as you exercise your leadership.

Keep in mind that identifying and articulating your values is usually not accomplished in one sitting. It takes a thoughtful evaluation of your purpose, convictions, and vision for the future. And, as you increasingly come to understand your inherent purpose and gifts, you should refine the written statement of your values.

2. Believe in Your Values

Values are not ideals to which a leader gives mere mental assent, because they are an indispensable part of his ability to live a life of purpose and character. Therefore, you should embrace values you can truly believe in and have confidence in—those you affirm and desire to live by.

3. Receive Your Values

A leader believes in his values to the point that he "receives" them. That is to say, he internalizes them, so they can become a vital part of who he is. You receive your values by reviewing them often, thinking about them, and affirming their place in your life. As King Solomon said, "As [a person] thinks in his heart [subconscious mind], so is he."

4. Live Out Your Values

As a result of the preceding steps, a true leader *adheres to* his values. They become his parameters, or framework, for living. A person of character measures everything against those parameters. For example, if you ask him to take some action or participate in a cause, he will evaluate whether doing so would be in alignment with his purpose and values. If not, he will decline.

As a leader, you must not only believe in and internalize your values but also put them into practice, if they are to guide your life. Periodically take time to evaluate if you are living according to your stated values.

5. Share Your Values

A leader must be able to share his values with others in the corporate entity of which he is a part—whether it is a family, a business, an organization, a nation, or another group. Remember that a personal vision can be fulfilled only in conjunction with other people's visions as they share a common purpose. Similarly, corporate values are effective only when they become the personal values of all the members. Every member of an organization needs to be in general agreement with the corporate values. We will discuss this point in more depth in a later chapter.

Therefore, if you are the leader who sets a corporate vision, you should remind people often of what is valuable to the community and what is valuable to you personally. These values should not be a secret to those who are involved. Values must not only be heard but also "seen"—in other words, demonstrated, especially by you.

If you study the life of Jesus of Nazareth, you will notice that He kept restating His values to His disciples and the crowds who came to hear Him speak—values concerning human life and human worth; values about what He considered of greatest significance. He said things like, "Seek first the kingdom of God and His righteousness."[3] By using the word "first," He was indicating priority. The kingdom of God, or the influence of heaven on earth, was what He valued above everything else. He believed that the kingdom of God would bring about the restoration of human beings and the reestablishment of the worth of every human life.

A leader must remind his followers often of what is valuable to the community and to him personally.

---

6. Allow Your Values to Motivate and Regulate Your Conduct and Policies

A leader's framework of values becomes his measure not only of *whether* he will do something but also *how* he will conduct himself while doing it. No matter what our values may be, they guide our behavior and our policies—both private and public.

Today, many leaders lack a framework for evaluating the suitability and consequences of their conduct and policies. Since values create character, a leader who does not have strong, positive values will be vulnerable to failing ethically and producing flawed policies. However, a leader who has established strong values for himself will exercise leadership that is ethically sound, as well as inspirational.

A Personal Commitment to Beliefs and Values

Let's consider again the case of Mahatma Gandhi. He challenged the powerful, well-established policies of the British Empire, by which it had made India its colonial territory, and he eventually enabled India to become an independent nation, free of British rule. Gandhi held certain values that he refused to give up—including his commitments to the equality of all people and to a policy of nonviolence—despite great pressure to conform, as well as other stresses and demands. He wasn't motivated by other people's approval of him, and he was willing to sacrifice his life for his beliefs.

Do you know how Gandhi's struggle for equality began? He was born and raised in India, and he studied law in Great Britain. Afterward, he traveled to South Africa to work as a lawyer. When he arrived, he bought a first-class train ticket, boarded a train, and sat down in his cabin.

The following is a paraphrased account of what occurred next. When the conductor came by to check the passengers' tickets, he looked at Gandhi and asked, "What are you doing in here?" Gandhi answered, "What do you mean? I paid to sit here." The conductor said, "No, you can't sit here." When he asked why, the man replied, "Because people like you are not supposed to sit in first class." He protested, "But I have a first-class ticket." "It doesn't matter what you have," he was told. "You aren't supposed to sit here. In South Africa, first class is only for white people."

In effect, the conductor was saying, "We don't value you as being equal to us." It was a value issue. When Gandhi refused to leave, the conductor called for security. Gandhi was pulled out of the seat that he'd paid for, and dragged off the train.

This denial of a value he held dear was the beginning of Gandhi's journey to becoming an inspirational leader who effected great change through the moral power of his beliefs and convictions. Again, it is hard to find leaders in our day who will refuse to relinquish their values in the face of pressure to compromise.

Today, many people give up their values because they want people to like them or because they fear recrimination or even physical harm. We are very "safety-conscious"; we don't want to upset anyone, and we don't want to have to sacrifice our time, our temporary pleasures, or our perceived reputations. Consequently, we accept circumstances and policies that we disagree with. We complain—but fail to act. As a result, we are of little use to our generation.

Leadership is not about comfort. It is about discomfort—discomfort with an ineffective, incomplete, or unjust status quo, and with one's own tendencies toward ease and complacency. Remember that whatever we accommodate, we will either embrace or be destroyed by.

True leaders have a personal commitment to their beliefs and values, and this is why they are willing to act when they see those beliefs and values violated. Remember the quotes from Abraham Lincoln and Nelson Mandela in chapter 2, in which they declared that they were willing to die for their beliefs? Sadly, many of us would not even be willing to get up a little earlier in the morning to pursue what we say we believe in and want to accomplish—let alone die for it.

Leadership is not about comfort but about discomfort with our desire for ease and complacency.

Ask yourself honestly, "What is the strongest motivation in my life and leadership right now?" Is it perhaps fame or status? What do you value more than your convictions? Is it money? Let me assure you that it would be much better for you to eat a slice of bread with your ethical convictions intact than to eat a juicy steak with compromise. Long after that steak dinner would have been forgotten, you would still remember the slice of bread you ate because you stood for what you believed in.

Life is short—you might as well live for something valuable!

What Values About Leadership Have We Accepted?

In the previous chapter, we discussed traditional philosophies that have contributed to the concepts of leadership many people hold today. To recap, these were (1) the "birth trait" theory, (2) the "chosen by the gods" theory, (3) the "charismatic personality" theory, and (4) the "external factors" theory—that leaders are born primarily through education or by dealing with certain situations with specific criteria and stimuli.

We will now examine three values that our culture has adopted in relation to leadership, as a result of our acceptance of these traditional philosophies. Consciously or subconsciously, we often consider the following values of leadership to be more important than character and the elements of character.

1. We Value Talent over Character

Many people regularly place their confidence in a leader's talents, above all other considerations. To understand the implications of this misplaced value, let's clarify the difference between talent and character.

+ Talent is a person's inherent gifts and abilities, as well as his skills, knowledge, and expertise.

+ Character is a person's personal submission to the discipline of adhering to principles that protect his talents and gifts.

As we have discussed, every human being is born with a unique gift or set of gifts. We gain additional skills, abilities, knowledge, expertise, and experience as we use our gifts and interact with the world, but the gifts themselves are innate. In contrast, we are not born with character. Some people's personalities may include a natural bent toward certain positive attributes, such as patience. But character must be intentionally valued and developed.

Overawed by Glamour

Too often, we allow ourselves to become so impressed with a person's talent that we choose to overlook his character flaws when making an investment in him as a leader. We must learn not to be overawed by spectacular talent. We can enjoy and appreciate someone else's gifts, but we should not expect his talent to be a reflection of the whole person.

There seem to be certain celebrities and politicians who continue to receive the public's approval and favor, no matter how discreditable their conduct. At such times, there are usually various reasons for this continued support. For example, in the case of a politician, one likely reason would be people's strong ties to a particular political party. Nevertheless, we live in a culture so enamored of famous people that the public often chooses to ignore their character defects, even though to do so is ethically unhealthy for both them and society.

Unfortunately, when we ignore the issue of character, we often reinforce in the minds of these leaders the perception that they will never be held responsible for their actions or for the poor examples they are setting. These leaders see that most people care only about their talent or appearance, and aren't concerned about whether they have moral standards. In this way, the public encourages them to disregard the development of their character—and may even contribute to their eventual downfall.

A Fickle Public

On the other hand, leaders should realize that the public can sometimes be very fickle about whom it admires. Certain individuals might be gifted, famous, and wealthy, but when their character defects come to light, they can instantly lose both popularity and favor. Suddenly, people no longer want to pay them money to exercise their gifts, or vote for them for public office, or buy tickets to be entertained by them. Why? The people felt betrayed when they realized that the gifted person's private life didn't correspond with his public persona. People often feel shocked and deceived when such revelations occur, because they have overemphasized the value of the person's talent, charisma, and glamour. They erroneously believe that people with these qualities should automatically have character, as well.

It is more important to be faithful than to be famous.

Some people take the position that a person's public life is not related to his private life (often because they don't think through their stance thoroughly enough). We'll explore the problems with this position in a later chapter. For now, we should remember that character is who we are when no one is watching. If you want to make an impact on the world with your leadership gifts, it is essential to shore up your gifts with strong character that can handle the pressures and temptations of life.

Talent Without Character

A person who has talent but lacks character can be unstable and unreliable. Some people have ability, but they don't have "availability." They're gifted, but they can't be counted on to contribute their gift consistently. Nothing is more frustrating to people who are involved in a joint endeavor—such as a business, a professional sports team, a film crew, a civic organization, or a college study group—than dealing with someone who is extremely talented but undependable. They cannot predict if the person will be present at the designated times to carry out his responsibilities. If he doesn't show up, their endeavor can be jeopardized.

Talent without character is like a shooting star. It shines brightly for a moment but then is gone. Sometimes, people come on the public scene who have a brilliant intellect, a sparkling personality, or dazzling good looks. They seem to have all the right ingredients for success. But then, sometime later—it may be two weeks, a year, or several years—they seem to drop out of sight, and we wonder where they went. We find out that they quickly "burned out" due to a character issue that destroyed their reputation and potential.

In contrast, character is like the sun—it shines consistently and reliably. At night, the sun illuminates another region of the world, even though we can't see it. On days when we experience cloudy skies or pouring rain, the sun is still shining from its consistent position in the solar system. People with character have these qualities of consistency and reliability. Consequently, they have a positive effect on the lives of those around them.

Distracted and Derailed

When leaders focus solely on their talent, ignoring issues of character, it can derail their purpose and distract other people from matters of true importance. Most people acknowledge that former U.S. president Bill Clinton was a good manager and a tremendous communicator. Whether they agree with his politics or not, they recognize his leadership abilities. Two of his accomplishments were balancing the federal budget and reducing the national debt.

Clinton was the most influential man on earth—a player on the world scene. He is well-educated and has talent and skills. I have met him on several occasions. If you were to walk into his presence, you would be disarmed, because he has powerful charisma. I believe that if someone who hated him talked with him for three minutes, he would end up liking him.

Yet while Clinton was president, his character flaw caused people to lose respect for him as a leader and brought him ridicule. It could even have cost him his position. Not only did he have sexual liaisons with a White House intern, but he also lied about it under oath, leading to his impeachment by the House of Representatives. The credibility of the most powerful man in the world was greatly damaged by his involvement with a young intern. Because of congressional and public uproar over his personal life, as well as the accompanying media frenzy, some of Clinton's policies and plans were hindered, and he and the country were unnecessarily distracted from national goals and concerns.

In my opinion, Clinton succumbed to one of the greatest dangers of leadership power and success—in essence, he believed he was above his own character. He was in such a position of power and authority that he thought his indiscretions would be shielded from discovery and protected from any consequences. That was a great personal deception. He didn't understand that he was only as safe as his character, and that protecting his character should have been one of his top priorities.

Because he allowed his character flaw to control him, no matter how much time passes, and no matter what other accomplishments he achieves, people will always remember the scandal that occurred during his presidency. His character defect and its aftermath are part of his permanent legacy. This is what happens when we value talent over character.

How would you like to be remembered?

2. We Value Reputation over Character

Another false value we have internalized is that a good reputation is more important than having genuine good character. We have made our public image a higher priority than our personal or corporate responsibleness. In doing so, we have failed to recognize the critical need to safeguard our integrity.

Let's examine the difference between reputation and character:

+ Reputation is what others think about you. Character is the truth about you.

+ Reputation is who you are in public. Character is who you are in private.

Each of us has a reputation—it is the perception other people have of us. People often "sell" an enhanced picture of themselves to others; they promote a public image that is not who they really are. Then, they sometimes start to believe the invention rather than the reality. It is ethically hazardous for us to be more concerned with what others think of us than with what we know to be true about ourselves.

Mere reputation does not have the ability to sustain you, because it is not based on reality. We should never trust our reputation, because it has the capacity to deceive us.

We must also avoid promoting a false image of ourselves, because life has a way of eventually bringing our private self to the public stage. Who you truly are will manifest itself somewhere along your life's journey, and it can destroy the image of "you" that others have bought into. Therefore, make sure you won't mind if who you are in private becomes public. Finally, remember this: Hardly anyone is able to die with his privacy intact.

> *Leaders should not seek to protect their reputation—*
> *they should seek to protect their character.*

Reputation is not something you have to pursue. It will be a by-product of your character. People will respect you for your character, so you never have to strive to maintain or protect your reputation. If your goal is to defend your reputation, you will move away from ethical considerations. Again, the best thing to do is to focus on maintaining your character and protecting your integrity. The more you develop your character, the less concerned you will be about your reputation.

3. We Value Position More Than Character

A third flawed value we have accepted is that position is more important than character—specifically, our disposition. By *disposition*, I mean a person's nature and outlook—including his sense of purpose and his self-concept. As we have discussed, an individual's position, rank, or status in an organization does not automatically equate to genuine leadership. Many people are more concerned with pursuing a high position in government, business, or the nonprofit sector than with having an honorable disposition. They choose to focus on outward status rather than on the quality of their inner life. I would much rather understand what motivates a person than hear what his latest title is, because his title really tells me very little about him.

One dictionary definition of *disposition* is "the tendency of something to act in a certain manner under given circumstances." That's a good description of character, too, one that we will look at more closely in a coming chapter. When we know someone's true character, we can usually predict what he will do in a given situation. That is vital knowledge to have about a leader or a potential leader.

Therefore, instead of seeking an elevated position in life, we should develop a strong disposition. We can begin by asking ourselves questions such as these:

+ Have I placed more value on my status or title than on my character?

+ What perceptions do I have about myself, other people, and the world? Are they aligned with my purpose? Do they reflect the values I claim to have?

+ What is my true nature, apart from my reputation?

+ What values will I refuse to deny because, to do so, I would violate my ideals and ethics?

Living Value-Directed Lives

As a result of the false ideas about leadership that our culture has accepted, we have too hastily given roles of leadership and responsibility to people without considering the ramifications of their turning out to be unprincipled leaders. For example, when we are looking for someone to head an organization, we usually choose someone on the basis of his experience and knowledge alone. (When we recognize that we are competent in a specific area, we often believe that this fact, in itself, qualifies us for leadership, too!) When we vote for someone for political office, we often choose someone just because he is well-known, well-spoken, or physically attractive. Yet focusing on these values exclusively, rather than seriously considering people's character, has done us and the world a great disservice. It has inevitably played a part in the ethical and moral scandals we are seeing among our leadership.

As leaders, we have a responsibility to live with utmost integrity. Our convictions must remain intact, no matter how much we may be tempted to compromise our honesty or to give in to our physical appetites. We must remember that people are looking to us and putting their faith in us. For the sake of our leadership, let us endeavor to live responsible lives based on strong values. We can do this as we identify, believe, receive, live out, and share our values, and as we allow them to motivate and regulate our conduct and policies.

5

How Character Develops, Part III: What We Serve

"For where your treasure is, there your heart will be also."[1]
—Jesus of Nazareth

We've been exploring the process of character development, which we could also refer to as our "philosophical journey"—how our beliefs, convictions, and values develop, as well as where they take us in life. Once we formulate our values, we translate them into specific personal moral standards, or principles, that express in what manner we will commit to live. The combination of our values comprises our personal standpoint, from which our morals are derived.

Moral Standards, or Principles

One dictionary definition of *moral* is "of or relating to principles of right and wrong in behavior." *Principle* can be defined as "a comprehensive and fundamental law, doctrine, or assumption." Moral standards, therefore, have to do with our beliefs about right and wrong behavior, based on the fundamental assumptions, or laws, that we have adopted.

True leaders esteem time-honored moral standards. Many contemporary leaders may recognize moral standards, but they do not esteem them. They do not hold them in high regard. How many leaders truly ask themselves, "Is this decision or opportunity that is open to me moral?" or, "Is what I'm about to do ethical?"

Unfortunately, people's concepts of "right" and "wrong" have become hazier today, contributing to the ethical crisis among our leaders. Yet, as we will see in chapter 7, this confusion often occurs as a mental or emotional response, more than as a response from the core of a person's inner being—the seat of his conscience, which responds to moral absolutes.

We must make a commitment to follow honorable principles. Leaders of character live by standards, not by expediency. Many people today are under great pressure to be expedient—to serve the needs or demands of a given moment or situation, rather than to serve their unique purpose in life and to do so according to moral standards. In my view, what we call "political correctness" is often a contemporary form of expediency that leads people to compromise their values.

Leaders of character live by standards, not by expediency.

Leaders are individuals who live by a set of principles that they will not compromise, even for the sake of expediency. They are able to do so because they have declared independence from the expectations of others. They are more concerned with manifesting their true selves than with "proving" themselves to others. In this regard, we could refer to a leader's commitment to time-honored principles as "ethical correctness." That should be the standard for twenty-first-century leaders.

Moral Standards Come from Within

Jesus of Nazareth said,

Don't you see that whatever enters the mouth goes into the stomach and then out of the body? But the things that come out of the mouth come from the heart, and these make a man unclean. For out of the heart come evil thoughts, murder, adultery, sexual immorality, theft, false testimony, slander.[2]

Immoral actions begin in the heart, or the subconscious mind. For example, individuals often practice lies before they tell them. People generally premeditate stealing, lying, committing adultery, or engaging in other unethical behavior. Then, they wait for an opportunity to do so, and when it arises, they take it. Some people may not specifically be "waiting" for an opportunity. However, they have imagined the act in their minds, and this weakens their willpower. Consequently, when the opportunity presents itself, they are much more likely to succumb, and actually do it.

In this sense, a thief was a thief before he stole something; a liar was a liar before he told an untruth. Everything a person does is rehearsed before it's manifested, because it comes from the core values and morals he has constructed for himself.

Moral Standards Are Personal Decisions

Being intentional about the moral standards by which we will live always involves making *personal decisions*. Standards are not just principles we think are "good ideas" we would do well to follow. Why? Because we can live our entire lives thinking that something is a good idea—but never follow it. So, moral standards are not just what we intellectually affirm to be right and beneficial; they are principles that we have made an active decision to follow.

Our beliefs determine our actions as they become our standards for living. Whatever we truly believe in, we will serve. This is a crucial point that each of us needs to take to heart: We must determine beforehand what we will serve. If we don't, we will allow our impulses, our circumstances, or other people's opinions to control us. We will never fulfill our leadership purpose and convictions if we haven't already decided to serve the values and moral standards that align with them and by which they can be accomplished.

It is easy for leaders to get caught in the trap of holding a double standard—not following the principles that they require or expect others to follow. For example, if parents are to exercise moral leadership in their homes, they must set an example for their children. Many young people today are frustrated because their parents expect them to behave according to ethical principles while the parents are engaging in unethical and immoral conduct—unsportsmanlike behavior, gossip, lying, cheating, abusing alcohol, and the like. Then parents wonder why, for instance, their daughter becomes pregnant at age thirteen, or their son gets arrested for drunk driving at age seventeen. They attempt to correct their children, when they themselves have allowed the children to become corrupted because they haven't instructed them in values or set a clear example of what it means to be an ethical leader.

Moral leadership doesn't always require many words. A principled leader can walk into a room of people and change the whole environment just by being there. Character has an atmosphere that goes with it. That is why I have said that character, or moral force, is the key to inspirational leadership. When you have moral force, you will inevitably inspire people. And that moral force comes from your convictions, which are translated into values and moral standards that set an example for others.

A principled leader can walk into a room of people and change the whole environment just by being there.

Examples of Personal Moral Standards

How can you establish moral standards for yourself? After you have developed a written statement of your values, you should also write down your personal principles for living. In the previous chapter, we discussed the example of a person who values the institution of marriage. Here is how that personal value could translate to a written moral standard for someone who is married: "I value the institution of marriage, so my corresponding personal moral standard, or principle for living, is that I will be faithful, and remain faithful, to my spouse."

We also used the example of esteeming the quality of honesty. Here is how that value could translate to a moral standard for a businessperson: "I esteem the quality of honesty; therefore, my corresponding moral conviction, or principle, is that I will always tell the truth to my customers and never overcharge them or bill them for services that were not performed."

Here is another example in relation to an individual who values the benefits of a strong and healthy physical body: "I value having a strong body that will enable me to live longer, be more productive, and enjoy life better. My corresponding moral conviction, or principle, is that I will maintain a fit body by regularly eating healthy foods and exercising, and by not abusing alcohol, drugs, or other addictive substances."

Discipline

Once we have determined our moral standards, written them down, and declared them to others, what does it take to keep them? We will explore this theme in more depth in a later chapter on how character is tested. But first, to be intentional about our character—following through with our established standards—requires exercising personal discipline. If we have genuine convictions, we will be motivated to discipline ourselves for the purpose of remaining aligned with those convictions.

Setting Priorities and Making Choices

Just as moral standards begin with our thinking, discipline begins with our mind. Being disciplined involves setting priorities for yourself that determine your choices and direct your behavior. Two dictionary definitions for *discipline* are "a rule or system of rules governing conduct or activity," or "orderly or prescribed conduct or pattern of behavior." When you have a "rule" that governs your activity, or when you have "prescribed" conduct for yourself, it means that you previously made some choices that you have determined will guide your activities and behavior.

Priorities are the key to effective decision-making. You must identify priorities in relation to achieving your vision and establishing the principles by which you will conduct your entire life, including how you will spend your time and money. Prioritizing places useful limits on your decisions—limits that will enable you to become the leader you were meant to be. You first determine what is beneficial for you, and then you order your life in ways that train and prepare you, and provide for the fulfillment of your purpose.

Self-imposed Parameters

The key to being disciplined is to set self-imposed parameters for your life in relation to both your moral standards and your daily activities— what you will and will not accept for yourself, and what you will and will not participate in. Are the activities you are currently involved in beneficial to your leadership purpose and vision? The choices we must make are not always between what is good and what is bad. Sometimes, they are between what is "good" and what is "better" or "best." Prioritizing protects you from trying to do everything. It keeps you from spending too much time on secondary pursuits.

Unless you establish moral standards and priorities for yourself, you will have no real beneficial restraints on your life. Therefore, ask yourself questions such as these:

+ On what am I expending my energies?

+ On what am I spending my money? Where am I investing my finances?

+ What am I feeding my mind and heart (TV shows, movies, books, music, Web sites) as a steady diet? Is what I am watching, reading, or listening to helping or hindering me in the pursuit of my purpose and vision? (All of the above types of resources are value-neutral—it is how they are used by others, and how we prioritize their use in our own lives, that makes the difference from a moral standpoint.)

+ What hobbies am I pursuing?

+ What food and other substances am I taking into my body?

+ What am I risking by my attitudes and behavior?

+ What am I neglecting to do that I should be doing?

Since personal discipline will enable you to remain aligned with your convictions, the above questions will help you to prioritize and to make good decisions for how to live your life.

Training Yourself and Setting the Pattern for Your Life

Let's look at two additional definitions of *discipline* that apply directly to our topic: "training that corrects, molds, or perfects the mental faculties or moral character," and "self-control." In chapter 1, I asked, "If you were tried in the court of your belief, would there be enough evidence to convict you?" I asked that question because, when you have faith in an idea or a moral standard to the point that you are willing to sacrifice for it, then we could say that you are a "convict" of it. Your belief system creates self-imposed parameters for your life, so that you will adhere to your principles.

A person of character "polices" himself, exercising self-control in accordance with his beliefs. When you have genuine conviction, you make sure you don't diverge from your chosen path. Once you have established strong standards, you don't permit your beliefs to stage a "jail break" and escape—no matter how much money someone offers you to compromise your convictions, or no matter what other short-term gain you might receive as a result.

There are many examples of leaders who became "convicts" of their philosophical ideas—whose belief systems created their convictions, which became the source of their moral positions and conduct. Rick Hodes, an American medical doctor, first went to Ethiopia in 1984 as a famine relief worker. While he was there, he developed the strong conviction that he belonged in that nation to serve the Ethiopian people through his skills as a physician. He moved to Ethiopia and, many years later, is still committed to that vision. Hodes reportedly "has served tens of thousands of people through immunization, family planning, community health, nutritional support and his specialist field—spine deformities." He has also adopted five Ethiopian children.[3]

Once you have established moral parameters for your life, you don't permit your beliefs to stage a "jail break" and escape.

Therefore, as a leader, you must protect your morals, because morals produce discipline in keeping with your convictions. They prompt you to impose constraints on yourself for the sake of a greater purpose. When you are committed to your beliefs and standards, no one else needs to put restrictions on you—you restrict yourself from what will hinder or harm you. You understand that there are purposes and goals in life that are immeasurably greater than temporary pleasures, secondary objectives, and everyday distractions.

True leaders live a very narrow life in relation to their purpose. They don't make room for much slackness; they are tough on themselves. Paul of Tarsus, the first-century leader, wrote to his Corinthian audience,

In a race all the runners run. But only one gets the prize. You know that, don't you? So run in a way that will get you the prize. All who take part in the games train hard. They do it to get a crown that will not last. But we do it to get a crown that will last forever. So I do not run like someone who doesn't run toward the finish line. I do not fight like a boxer who hits nothing but air. No, I train my body and bring it under control. Then after I have preached to others, I myself will not break the rules and fail to win the prize.[4]

Paul exercised self-discipline, and he encouraged those whom he was leading to do the same. He spoke of being intentional about "training hard." Notice that he did so for the purpose of reaching his goal, which he described as "the prize." He knew he would not fulfill his purpose unless he disciplined his life. Accordingly, I encourage you to add a statement of your priorities, choices, and self-imposed parameters to your written record of your beliefs, convictions, values, and moral standards.

Remember that one of the definitions of *discipline* is "prescribed pattern of behavior." Personal discipline in line with moral standards manifests in a pattern of ethical conduct. Similarly, immoral or unethical conduct by an individual—in which, for example, an individual ignores his convictions for the sake of temporary pleasure—is evidence of a lack of discipline in his life. When an absence of discipline becomes a negative *pattern* in a leader's life, he is in danger of such consequences as constant frustration, ineffectiveness, personal and financial setbacks, and moral failure. Our moral standards, or principles, can't become established within us unless we discipline ourselves, so that they become a positive pattern of behavior in our lives.

Ethics

This leads us to the next stage of character development, in which our conduct and/or disciplined actions manifest as our ethics. Let's look at several dictionary definitions of *ethics*, in which I have emphasized certain words in boldface type: "a **set** of moral principles: a theory or **system** of moral values," "the **principles** of conduct governing an individual or a group," or "a **guiding philosophy**."

In previous chapters, we've talked about leaders establishing a "code of ethics." A code of ethics brings together what we've discussed over the past three chapters. It is the synthesis of a leader's beliefs, convictions, values, and moral standards, as well as the priorities and choices that determine his personal discipline. A code of ethics is a clearly delineated guiding philosophy and system of moral principles to which he commits in order to exercise effective, ethical leadership.

An individual's experience of exercising leadership will be much easier—and more fulfilling—if he establishes strong beliefs and convictions, and determines his values, moral standards, and priorities at the beginning of the process of his leadership development. Yet all of us must continually work to strengthen the areas of ethical weakness in our lives, and to develop the qualities of principled leaders. Our code of ethics is like a compass, pointing us to the goal we are moving toward. In the end, the quality of our character depends on the nature and durability of our ethical code.

Our code of ethics is the synthesis of our beliefs, convictions, values, moral standards, priorities, and discipline.

Character Controls Lifestyle

Lastly, the conduct that we manifest, as a result of our commitment to our code of ethics (or our lack of such), defines our character. And our character controls our lifestyle. That is where our philosophical journey ultimately leads—it determines the entire shape and scope of our lives. In this sense, we could say that our character *is* our life.

Addressing Deficiencies in Character Development

Now that we've explored the process of character development, let's discuss what can be done when we realize that we've allowed certain negative character traits to become established in our lives. If we have flaws in our belief system (and we all have them), some of our convictions and values will be faulty, resulting in gaps or failings in the course of our personal development. As we have seen, none of us "receives" character issues from someone or something outside of us. They come from within us—from our heart, or subconscious mind.

Once you have identified character flaws in your life, you must immediately begin to correct them. To identify the source of a character flaw, you need to discover where the defect occurred in the process of your development. Usually, this means rebuilding areas of your philosophy, substituting your faulty beliefs and convictions with solid ones.

Ideally, defects that appear during the process of an individual's character development should be corrected lovingly but firmly by his parents or grandparents, or perhaps teachers or other mature adults in his community. If these defects are not addressed, they will magnify in the person's life, and they may eventually manifest as a massive character disaster. The sooner a person learns how to intentionally develop strong values, moral standards, and discipline, the better—for his own sake, and for the benefit of society.

As I wrote earlier, a leader's character defects will frequently manifest when he is given power, position, and/or wealth. At any level of leadership, most leaders have one or more of these resources, to some degree. The saying "Absolute power corrupts absolutely" is not entirely correct. It is not the power itself but something within a person that corrupts him and causes him to misuse his power and abuse other people.

If a person had absolute power, he could use it to be a blessing to other people. Some leaders who have had great power have used it for that purpose. Power is not a problem unless it is used by someone who lacks character. The same principle applies to wealth. There's nothing wrong with money itself—the problem is the manner in which a person handles and controls it, which is tied to his character. Power, authority, position, money, influence, and so forth are meant to be tools that enable a leader to achieve a noble purpose—not to serve selfish or dishonorable ends.

A Paradox of Strengths and Weaknesses

I mentioned previously that most people have certain positive traits and certain negative traits—strengths and weaknesses of character. The

Bible provides some very interesting character studies in this regard. The life of King David is a fascinating paradox that manifests moral strengths and weaknesses alike. As a young man, David held strong convictions that lifted him into the highest position of leadership and made him into a great ruler. However, after he received power, certain character defects manifested in the way he used that power.

Let's first look at an incident that reveals one of David's convictions, which led to his exercising ethical leadership. David had been anointed to be the next king of Israel. He had once been close to the current king, Saul, but the king had become increasingly jealous of him and sought to kill him. David had been forced to flee for his life.

At one point, circumstances gave David an opportunity to kill Saul when the king entered a cave, not realizing that David and his men were hidden in the shadows at the very back of the cavern. David's men urged him to kill Saul, and David crept up quietly to the king and cut off a corner of his robe (perhaps as a symbol of taking over Saul's reign). Immediately, David regretted his action. The idea that he had even considered killing the king caused him to be conscience-stricken—despite the fact that Saul was trying to kill him. This was because David held a deep conviction that Saul was the "anointed of the Lord," and David was still Saul's subject.

When Saul left the cave, David followed and called out to him, telling him that he had spared his life and that he meant him no harm. He quoted an old saying to the king as he explained, "'From evildoers come evil deeds,' so my hand will not touch you."[5] Saul continued to pursue David, and David had a second opportunity to kill him one night when the king and his men were sound asleep in their camp. Yet he again spared Saul's life.

Saul was eventually killed in battle against the Philistine nation. David then became king over all of Israel—without forcing his way into the position, which would have established his kingship on the wrong foundation from the start.[6] To quote a proverb later written by Solomon, David's son and successor, "Such is the end of all who go after ill-gotten gain; it takes away the lives of those who get it."[7]

David's response to Saul is in striking contrast to the subsequent behavior of David's son Absalom, who was hungry for power and attempted to overthrow his father's throne. Absalom was eventually killed (contrary to David's orders), and David mourned the loss of his son.[8]

"Ill-gotten gain...takes away the lives of those who get it."

Because of his convictions and moral standards, David had exercised personal restraint in preserving Saul's life. Yet, sometime after he had been established as king, he compromised his moral standards for the sake of temporary pleasure one evening when he became enamored of a beautiful woman. Even though he knew she was married to one of his loyal soldiers, he sent messengers to bring her to his palace, and he had sexual relations with her. Later, when she sent him a message saying that she was pregnant, he arranged to have her husband killed in battle. Then, he brought her to the palace permanently as his wife.[9]

Somewhere along the way of his character development, he allowed a flaw to form that manifested in adultery when he was in a position to arrange to indulge in it—and then to commit murder to cover it up—thinking that his actions could be kept secret. But they eventually came to light. When David was confronted about his actions, he fully admitted to them, acknowledging the path that had led to his immoral conduct. While he remained king, he suffered consequences.[10]

As we saw earlier, a similar defect occurred at some point during President Clinton's philosophical journey that influenced his values and resulted in a flaw in his character. He had not committed to the principle that adultery is a moral violation, and even afterward, he continued to justify his unethical actions in his own mind.

When Sleeping Snakes Are Awakened

Character defects are like sleeping snakes that awaken and strike people when they enter positions of leadership and receive the trappings of power. As I wrote earlier, character failure often occurs when a person is in the midst of success. In many ways, success is the greatest test of character. This is because most people cannot handle success—they are not prepared for it, and the weight of it becomes too heavy for them. As a result, some area of their character collapses. Many wonderful, gifted people have crumbled under the burden of success.

Yet when a leader has committed to a code of ethics, it will protect him by eliminating "sleeping snakes." It will become a continual reminder of his prescribed conduct and self-imposed parameters, which he has determined to abide by for the sake of achieving and preserving his vision.

You're Not Finished Yet!

The concepts of these last few chapters, and of this entire book, are ones that I have thought about and researched for more than thirty years. I urge you not to take what I've written lightly. It could save your leadership and your life over the next ten or twenty years. Remember that no matter how great a leader you become, you could lose everything that you've gained due to a lack of character.

Regardless of what you've already accomplished, you're not finished yet. Never become impressed by your prior accomplishments, because they can hold you back from achieving even higher ones. The greatest enemy of progress is your last success. Rejoice over it for a few days, and then move on. Press on to new heights, holding fast to your principles, so that your leadership will not be cut short by moral or ethical failure.

Don't forfeit your leadership in the midst of your growth and success as a leader. Make sure you prepare yourself by developing morally and ethically as a human being. Success is part of leadership, but it must be carried by character.

6

The Role of Values in Corporate Life

*"Leadership is the wise use of power. Power is the capacity to
translate intention into reality and sustain it."*
—Warren G. Bennis, leadership expert and author

A popular television show depicts what life would be like in the world,
particularly in America, if suddenly all the electrical power went
out—and no one could turn it back on again. While the TV show is fiction, the problem it portrays is a reality for many people in certain regions
of the world, including the country of Nigeria.

Several years ago, while on a speaking trip to Nigeria, I was talking with a
top lawyer in that nation who was one of my hosts. I inquired, "Nigeria is the
seventh-largest oil producer in the world, but most Nigerians don't have electricity. Everywhere I go, people use generators for power. There is no national
grid in place to run electricity to people. Explain that to me." He said, "Well,
it's not in the best interests of the politicians for the people to have electricity.
Every time they discuss that issue in the parliament, they vote it down."

When I asked why government leaders would vote down giving people
access to electricity, he replied, "Most of the politicians own either generator companies or companies that prepare them or provide fuel for them."
Because the politicians had a particular business interest, the majority of
their country's citizens were being denied a key resource for their lives.

Perhaps you, too, live in a nation where corruption or mismanagement is holding back resources or improvements from its people. When I became aware of the underlying problem in Nigeria, I knew I could not address the issue directly, because it was a symptom of a greater issue—an apparent lack of values among many of the nation's leaders. Therefore, when I had the opportunity to speak to a number of these leaders, I talked about character and how it affects national life. I knew that when leaders catch a vision of character, they begin to change their values and their conduct. Subsequently, their values become their policies.

Slowly, the situation has begun to change in Nigeria. There have been efforts to reform and privatize the electric industry. But there are still many internal challenges, and there have been setbacks. Reportedly, 120 million people in that nation, or *three quarters* of the population, still do not have access to electricity.[1] But leaders are continuing to work on the problem. Such issues require commitment and perseverance, as well as the development of shared values among the leaders and citizens.

When leaders catch a vision of character,
they begin to change their values and their conduct;
subsequently, their values become their policies.

Corporate Influence

As a leader, always be aware of this reality: Your personal values and moral principles have a significant influence on those who participate with you in your corporate effort, as well as others who are affected by your policies and conduct. I use the word *corporate* here to refer to any form of association or joint effort, on any level—families, nonprofit organizations, churches, businesses, local communities, county or regional governments, states or provinces, nations, coalitions of nations, and so forth.

You set the tone for your followers. Your leadership role and its influence include some or all of the following:

+ Maximizing the corporate vision.

+ Transforming the corporate culture to the point that your personal beliefs, attitudes, standards, and behavior are adopted by your followers or constituents.

◆ Establishing policy, or the regulations and laws that govern your constituents.

◆ Determining the direction, security, and prosperity of the group.

◆ Setting standards in relation to corporate ethics and intended outcomes.

◆ Effecting change.

These are substantial responsibilities, and it is essential to know how the corporate values that you establish and promote will impact the ethical environment and success of your endeavor. Additionally, although you are a leader in the realm of your own gifting, you are also a member of other corporate entities whose values exert influence on you. Are you aware of the impact they are having on you? Moreover, what responsibilities do you have as a participant in these groups?

For example, you are the citizen of a nation. Do you know the vision and values of your country? Are its values constant, or are they shifting? What influence do these values exert on you? What are your commitments to your nation?

You may also be a member of a community organization, such as a volunteer group. Are you aware of its purpose and values? Could you express them to someone else? Do you agree with them? What are your responsibilities in relation to this group?

In this chapter, we will look at the vital role that values play in corporate life. We will further explore how to apply to our particular leadership situations what we've learned about values and morals over the last few chapters, and we will discover how corporate values influence our own lives.

Values and Corporate Life

As I wrote in chapter 1, leaders have always fulfilled a central role in human life. Organizations, communities, societies, and nations are founded, established, and maintained by leaders. People look to leaders for direction, and they listen to their views. Even when a leader is wrong, many people still think he is right, simply because he is a leader. Additionally, what a leader values usually determines how a group functions.

Corporate Entities Have Character

Each corporate body manifests a distinct character, just as each human being does. And, as is the case with individuals, that character can be either positive or negative. It all depends on what values the group holds. If an individual leads a group long enough, his character will eventually permeate the community. As a corporate entity is directed by its leader/executive/supervisor/administrator, it manifests particular beliefs, convictions, values, and moral principles. It may also manifest ethical flaws and their consequences—sometimes on a large scale. For example, a business's motivation for creating its products, as well as the manner in which it creates them, is related to its corporate values. Values, morals, and ethics are clearly significant on a corporate level, just as they are in the life of an individual.

If an individual leads a group long enough, his character will eventually permeate the community.

Corporate Values Should Be Intentional

Leaders have an indispensable role in the development of corporate culture. Every leader of a common endeavor should be intentional about establishing positive values that will govern how the members function—with honesty, respect for others, a conscientiousness about quality, a commitment to providing excellent service, an eagerness to be productive, and so forth. Good character can be developed through careful training, but it can also deteriorate through neglect. A leader should not only personally adopt strong values, moral standards, discipline, and an ethical code, but he should also encourage the group's members to do so.

Principles of Corporate Values

In chapter 4, we defined values in this twofold way:

+ Ideas, principles, and qualities on which you personally place high worth.

+ Standards or ideals that determine your conduct or policy.

Let's see at how these definitions apply in a collective context by looking at several principles of corporate values.

1. Values Are the Foundation of a Corporate Entity

Corporate values shape the lives and daily experiences of the members, sometimes in profound ways. These values can take the form of (1) core ethical values that become moral standards and disciplines; and (2) specific ideas and approaches upon which the organization places high worth and on which it has chosen to focus.

Core Ethical Values

We know that an individual's values are derived from his beliefs and convictions. In a similar way, a corporate entity's values develop from the beliefs and convictions of the leader and the group members, which are based on their purpose. A group's values are the source of its character. For example, a nation's laws, which reflect its character, should be derived from the core values of its people; these laws should then be guarded and enforced by its leaders.

An organization's core values are the guiding principles by which it is committed to achieve its vision. The "core" of a person or thing is the place from which its energy emanates. Therefore, the core values of an organization, a business, or a country are its center of control. They control its associations, moral standards, discipline, and environment.

If a corporate entity's ideals and standards are based on solid principles, they will minimize and contain incidences of corruption within the organization. Conversely, in unprincipled corporate entities, corruption will be unconstrained. In the case of a nation, if the leaders do not value honesty, justice, and respect for the weakest of their citizens, there will be corruption and abuse throughout the country's system of government.

The Red Cross is an example of an organization whose strong values are based on its convictions. Its stated mission is "compassionate care to those in need...preventing and relieving suffering, here at home and around the world." It holds the conviction that every human life is worth saving, protecting, and helping. It doesn't matter who the person is; if he is in need, the Red Cross wants to help him. The organization has demonstrated its values by, among other outreaches, providing international assistance in seventy countries and working to "meet the needs of the world's most vulnerable communities."[2]

A corporate entity's core values are the guiding principles
by which it is committed to achieve its vision.

Specific Ideas and Focuses

Let's look now at the second definition of corporate values, in which an organization has specific ideas and approaches upon which it places high worth, and on which it has chosen to focus. For instance, in the business world, each company reflects distinct characteristics. Rolls-Royce is unique among automobile manufacturers. Its vision is not just to produce cars. Rather, it is to create an "experience" of driving. To achieve this vision, the company builds every car by hand. "A pioneering spirit and a sense of adventure define Rolls-Royce," the company says on its Web site, where consumers can read background stories about its "legendary" models.[3]

People can buy a functional car from almost any automobile company. If they want to be purely pragmatic—and many consumers do—they can buy a much less expensive car that runs well. But if a customer is looking for unique performance and custom features, he will go to a Rolls-Royce dealer or another high-end car company because of the specific value it places on bespoke workmanship.

The quality of a car is a manifestation of the character of the individuals who built it—and the character of these individuals reflects the overall values and character of the company they work for. Those who are employed by a particular company abide by corporate values that may be distinct from the corporate values of other companies. For example, if your job was to oversee the installation of seats in Rolls-Royce cars, you couldn't focus solely on the mechanics of the installation—you would have to make sure your performance contributed to the "experience" for the consumer, by your personal care of the product and your fine attention to detail.

Similarly, corporate values can indicate ideas that are important to one group but not to another related group. To use the example of automobiles again, one company may value speed of production more than quality of goods produced. The former was a value that many American car companies appeared to embrace a number of years ago. Their primary value seemed to be getting as many cars as possible through the assembly line, as quickly as possible. Quality took a "backseat." Essentially, the idea was, "We want to assemble vehicles faster and at less cost. So, we'll use cheaper parts, and we won't be as concerned about quality, in order to make more money."

In contrast, the values of Japanese companies seemed to include producing well-made cars that would last a long time, run well, and require fewer repairs. The car industries of two different countries were manufacturing the same mode of transportation but under distinct value systems. In the end, the companies who prized quality won out among consumers, forcing their rival companies to focus more on quality, as well. This gave consumers more choices when looking for reliable transportation.

In relation to all companies, we can—and should—ask ourselves, "What are the values and character of this business? How does its character compare to other companies that make a similar product?" We can ask similar questions of all forms of corporate entities.

2. A Corporate Entity Must Promote Positive Values to Function Well

Corporate bodies have to promote and protect positive values in their community if it is to function well, maintain its viability, and thrive.

Society, or the "National Community"

For instance, society—the "national community" of a country—must support values like cooperation, honesty, and trust, or it will decline. For the community's well-being, these values have to be found among its citizens and those with whom the citizens interact. The national community must work to preserve its cherished values, and its leaders must endeavor to protect those values in various ways for the sake of its members. The community comes to rely on those positive values in order to function. (When a nation's leaders and/or citizens do not esteem and protect positive values, the community will become oppressed and demoralized—a situation that has occurred in various nations throughout history, such as the former Soviet Union and North Korea.) Let's look at a few illustrations related to values of trust and safety in the context of communities that esteem positive values.

When a member of a society buys a bottle of water from a business within that society, he places faith in that business, as well as the manufacturer, that the water is safe for him to drink. The consumer hasn't witnessed the bottling process personally, and the bottle is sealed, so he can't test it for contamination before he purchases it. He has to trust that the business is offering bottled water from a reputable company. And, he has to have faith that this company has character—that what it states on its label concerning the contents of its product is truthful.

Some countries have instituted safety ordinances, holding companies accountable to live up to the standards that the national community has established for the welfare and protection of its citizens. As a corporate entity, the United States of America has created agencies such as the Food and Drug Administration (FDA), whose motto (value) is "Protecting and Promoting *Your* Health"[4] and whose task is to monitor the quality of the food and drink that are offered for sale to the nation's people.

The "national community" of a country must support values like cooperation, honesty, and trust, or it will decline.

Another example of corporate trust is the confidence that members of a society place in their banks. When people make deposits, they have faith that their money will still be there when they want to make a withdrawal. If a bank is reputable, its guarantee that the money will be kept safe and available is one of its corporate values, which it extends to its depositors. There is a legal and moral transaction between an individual and his bank anytime he makes a deposit or utilizes the bank's other financial services.

Many national communities maintain programs to ensure that the society's values are upheld in such financial dealings. Years ago, the United States government created the Federal Deposit Insurance Corporation (FDIC). If a depositor's funds are held in a participating bank, his money is insured for up to $250,000; these funds are guaranteed if the financial institution should fail. Although the FDIC was established by the government, it is not funded by it. It is financed primarily by the insurance premiums that member banks pay to the agency. Banks take part in this program in order to show good faith to their depositors and to protect their own values and reputation in the community.[5]

Even so, large banks or other lenders sometimes experience massive failures, such as we saw happen during the global economic downturn of 2007–08 and the years following. A lending institution's failure may result from the reckless investments or unethical practices of its executives. Yet, even in such cases, the U.S. government may still authorize "bailouts" of banks, in order to cover depositors' funds that are above the insured amount. (Other governments have taken similar action.) It does so for the purpose of protecting the economy—and, ultimately, the community's values of trust and safety.

These bailouts are usually controversial, since the money for them *does* come from the government—through the taxpayers. In this way, certain members of the national community sometimes end up paying for the mistakes and unethical conduct of other members of the national community, often causing the first group to feel that they have been taken advantage of. Under such circumstances, the national community's bond—based on mutual cooperation, honesty, and trust—can begin to break down. Leaders of all fields and industries must therefore seek to abide by strong core values, keeping the crucial relationship of mutual trust in their societies strong.

Business

It is not just national communities but also other corporate bodies, such as civic organizations and individual businesses, that depend on values like integrity, honor, fairness, and respect in order to function. Let us look at some examples from the world of business. Suppose you are hired by a company, with the agreement that you will be paid every two weeks. To enter into such an agreement, you have to accept the company's word that it will compensate you for your work. You have to trust that your employer is going to give you a paycheck for the negotiated amount every other Friday. Likewise, the company has to trust that you will perform the agreed-upon work. This is an exchange of integrity and honor between the company and its employee. You have entered into a mutual contract on the basis of specifically stated or implied values of trustworthiness.

In another example, when you go to a car dealer to buy a new or used automobile, you have to trust that what the salesperson says about the car is true. People trust salespeople all the time, even though they may joke about the stereotypical "crooked used-car salesman." In the case of new cars, manufacturers provide warranties guaranteeing certain repairs and maintenance for a given number of years or a specified mileage. These warranties are reflections of the companies' value of accountability. They are one method by which the company works to maintain association with its dealers and its customers, new and repeat alike.

In the case of a used car, you might be able to review the car's service history, or you might arrange to have a mechanic inspect the vehicle. But you still may not know everything about the condition of the car. Therefore, if you make a final decision to purchase it, you have to do so with a degree of trust. Regardless of the ultimate trustworthiness of a product, trust is a necessary part of sale transactions.

To strengthen consumer confidence, thus supporting values of honesty and fairness in their society, citizens have created various nonprofit organizations that promote trust, integrity, and fairness in business. One such organization is the Better Business Bureau, whose mission is "to be the leader in advancing marketplace trust."[6]

"Seven Social Sins"

Because corporate entities must rely on values to function, it is necessary for nations, businesses, nonprofit groups, families, and so forth to work to ensure that strong values are promoted and protected within their own group. We have looked at some examples of how nations and organizations have done this. But what happens when strong ethical values *aren't* protected and promoted within a corporate entity? Mahatma Gandhi published a list of "seven social sins" in his newspaper *Young India* in 1925 that provides a vivid picture of a society deficient in values and morals.

1. Wealth without work

2. Pleasure without conscience

3. Knowledge without character

4. Commerce without morality

5. Science without humanity

6. Worship without sacrifice

7. Politics without principles

To these seven, I would add an eighth:

8. Action without accountability

A Perpetual Problem

The above ways of conducting life can destroy a society. We should realize that a breakdown of ethics in a community will become a perpetual problem unless there is some intervention. When leaders are unethical, they negatively influence the people, and, sooner or later, the culture becomes infected with unethical behavior. Then, new leaders emerge who have been brought up in that culture and therefore mirror its lack of ethics. They, in turn, negatively influence the people, and so on.

Ironically, after these new leaders are elected or appointed, their constituents often expect them to suddenly be wiser and more ethical than they were beforehand. The people somehow expect a miracle of transformation to happen between the election/appointment of the person and the time he begins to exercise the responsibilities of his office. (This phenomenon is one evidence of human beings' inherent moral sense of right and wrong, which we will investigate in the next chapter.) Yet leaders produced by a culture that is pervaded with a lack of values will have a similar lack of values. They will be no wiser or more moral than the general public.

Occasionally, there are exceptions to this general rule. Sometimes, we encounter extraordinary people who almost seem to have been born with a strength of character that causes them to rise higher than the ethics of their environment. But such leaders are rare, and all of them would likely affirm that they still had to intentionally work on cultivating their character.

Monitoring and Protecting Values

Considering the moral and ethical decline of societies around the globe today, we must take seriously the need for character development. It has to begin with individual leaders, like ourselves, and we have to promote character on a grassroots level—since, as we've discussed, leaders are produced by their culture. This is why we must encourage the teaching of character development in our leadership training courses and schools. The culture itself has to be changed—one person at a time—if moral character is to be fully established among our leaders.

Values are integral to national and social development. When the leaders and citizens of a country begin to place less worth on the foundational values that once held their nation together, the country starts to lose its character. All nations must decide what values they will monitor, protect, and maintain.

In America and other nations today, leaders are tampering with core values—either adjusting them or rejecting them outright. In expressing their opposition to these changes, some of the spiritual leaders in the Western world have said, "We're moving away from traditional values." By using the term "traditional values," they are expressing this idea: "We've relied on various core values for hundreds of years. Now, we are debating moving away from them and relying on different values, which means that we are going to change the essence of our country."

Changing a national core value is beneficial only when doing so will realign a country with what is true and just. Often, other changes are detrimental because they contribute to a breakdown of moral standards. When considering the role of core values, the question is, "Do you want to change the core beliefs and values of your country to the point that it takes on an altogether different character?" If half of the citizens say yes to this question, and half say no, a nation is in serious trouble, because the people cannot agree about what they consider of greatest worth to the community as a whole.

A society must monitor and protect what it values,
because its values become its character.

---

3. A Corporate Entity's Values May Be Unspoken yet Recognized

A third principle is that values do not have to be explicitly stated in order to exist in a community. For example, in many nations, there is an unspoken value that younger men and women who are seated on a bus or another form of public transportation will stand up and allow an elderly person to sit down, as a courtesy. This value is no longer universally followed in some societies. However, the people who do observe it probably accepted it as an unspoken value when they were children, by watching the conduct of their parents and other adults. In some families and societies, this practice is still specifically taught.

Let's look at another example of an unspoken value, in the context of business transactions. Suppose someone took his clothes to a dry cleaner. The individual shop may or may not have a prominent sign guaranteeing its work. Yet even if it doesn't, the customer relies on the unspoken value connected with doing business that he is going to get his clothes back, and they are going to be clean. If the dry cleaner violated this unspoken value, especially more than once, the association between the customer and the shop would be broken. This simple example demonstrates that shared values—even unspoken ones—are necessary for continued relationship in any corporate entity.

How Corporate Values Function

Keeping in mind the above principles, let's explore what is required for values to operate successfully in a corporate body.

1. Core Values Must Be Communicated Clearly

Members of a corporate entity should be fully aware of the values of the community and be periodically reminded of them, so that the values remain clear and in the forefront of their minds. In a previous section, we talked about the role of the Federal Deposit Insurance Corporation (FDIC) in protecting consumers from bank failures. On its Web site, the FDIC plainly states its mission, its vision, and its six core values. I have included its core values below as a good model of what written corporate values look like:

+ **Integrity:** We adhere to the highest ethical and professional standards.

+ **Competence:** We are a highly skilled, dedicated, and diverse workforce that is empowered to achieve outstanding results.

+ **Teamwork:** We communicate and collaborate effectively with one another and with other regulatory agencies.

+ **Effectiveness:** We respond quickly and successfully to risks in insured depository institutions and the financial system.

+ **Accountability:** We are accountable to each other and to our stakeholders to operate in a financially responsible and operationally effective manner.

+ **Fairness:** We respect individual viewpoints and treat one another and our stakeholders with impartiality, dignity, and trust.[7]

All corporate entities should establish stated values that communicate their character and expectations. For example, a company might post a sign in several prominent locations in its building that says "As a company, we are not interested in only your gifts—we are interested in your good character." If an employee has exceptional gifts but lacks character, he may engage in unethical and/or illegal acts—like stealing from the company. For example, a personal assistant might be able to type over 100 words per minute, but if he is dishonest, he may take a computer home one day and never bring it back. I've seen similar things happen.

2. Core Values Require Total Corporate Commitment

In any corporate entity, there has to be a general agreement among the members about what values have high worth and therefore must be upheld and preserved. Otherwise, there will be disorder and confusion, as well as a breakdown of unity, as we have discussed. Every member of an organization should concur with, and be governed by, the corporate values.

3. Core Values Must Become the Personal Values of the Individual Members

This point is related to number 2, but it reflects the idea that although corporate affirmation of values is essential, values can be fully effective only when they are personally embraced by the individual members of the group. Remember that an individual's personal vision is always found in the context of a larger corporate vision. If a member doesn't see how his personal vision may be fulfilled within the corporate vision—if what he values most isn't aligned with that corporate vision—he will become detached from the rest of the group, and the quality of his contribution will diminish. In such a case, it is not necessarily a problem of unethical standards. The individual may have the same moral principles as the rest of the group, but what he values in terms of his purpose, and how he would like to fulfill it, differs from the vision and goals of the rest of the community.

How is the vision of a corporate entity protected? It is protected by the participants' shared values, accompanied by common moral standards— whether written or implied—discipline, and ethics. A corporate standard will mean nothing if the members don't accept it as their personal standard. When they don't, they become a drain on the organization; they begin to undermine its purpose. Values always originate with individuals' beliefs and convictions. Then they are applied to corporate arenas. The personal and the corporate must align.

When a member isn't aligned with the corporate vision,
he will become detached from the rest of the group,
and the quality of his contribution will diminish.

Corporate Responsibility and Personal Responsibility

I remember hearing about an incident in which an aircraft had to make an emergency landing because one of the engine plates had not been locked properly before a flight, causing a dangerous and potentially life-threatening situation. As I understand it, if an engine plate falls off a plane in midair at 300 mph, it can become like a razor-sharp knife able to cut right through steel.

During the investigation of the incident, people in the media were asking, "Who is at fault here?" The discussions I heard on television were interesting in light of corporate values. One person said, "First of all, the pilot should have checked for that while doing his walk-around of the plane." It is routine for a pilot to check specific items before a flight. So when a pilot walks around an aircraft, he isn't just stretching his legs; he's looking at various aspects of the plane, double-checking the work that the maintenance crew has performed.

The television commentators then asked, "Did the captain fail to check it? Or was it the fault of maintenance?" Any individual who performs maintenance on a plane has to sign off on a checklist of items. The authorities knew which individuals had been involved with the maintenance of the plane. Had they failed to close the plate properly? The commentators went on to say, "The supervisor is then supposed to sign off on what the maintenance crew signed off on."

As I listened to this ongoing commentary about the plane incident, my conclusion was that it was a corporate values issue. Even though it was determined that someone on the maintenance crew had neglected to lock the plate correctly, the fault came down to a company issue, not an individual one. Everyone connected with the airline was supposed to personally accept what the company had agreed upon as its corporate values—including those related to safety. That means the pilot had to do his part during his walk-around; the maintenance crew had to do its part and not sign off until it had checked all the details, such as whether the engine plates had been locked properly; the supervisor had to make sure the maintenance crew had done its job; and so on. Everyone has to work together toward corporate success. And working together means having common values.

A Realigning of Values

When someone becomes a member of an organization, he may find it necessary to adjust some of his core values so that they align with the core values of the group. Suppose someone seeking employment interviews with a corporation and reads on the job application a list of the company's core values, one of which is teamwork. The candidate realizes that, up to this point in his career, he has been very independent-minded. One of his values has been to work on his own rather than with a team.

The candidate has two choices. He can retain his former value of working alone and try to find a position where he can do so at a different company. Or, he may decide that working with others to some degree is a necessary component in any endeavor and is a value he would like to develop. In that case, he can decide to embrace the company's value and adhere to it if he is hired.

In another example, suppose a citizen of one nation immigrates to a different country and wants to become a citizen there. The governing articles of the new country delineate certain core values that reflect its character. Because the immigrant wants to become a citizen of that society, it becomes necessary for him to accept its stated core values. In fact, many people are motivated to move to a new country and take up citizenship there because they are especially drawn to its values.

A new citizen could, of course, merely pretend to have a commitment to his adopted nation's values. If he does, he weakens the unity among the members of that society. He might even become a danger to them, if he wanted to actively attack those values. To become a committed and meaningful member of his country, a new citizen must personally adhere to its foundational beliefs. Relatedly, if all the citizens of a country made a commitment to actively embrace the ethical values that the national community espoused, then ethical and moral corruption would quickly diminish.

When someone joins a group, he may need to adjust his core values so that they align with the core values of the organization.

Let's look at a third example. Suppose a young person has just graduated from high school. His parents allow him to live at home rent free, so he finds a part-time afternoon job. Then, he spends the summer staying up late with his friends every night and sleeping until eleven o'clock in the morning. At first, he is happy with this arrangement; he values the lack of demands in his unstructured existence. Soon, however, he realizes that his life isn't going anywhere. After looking at his options, he decides to join the army. In making this choice, he has to change his value system from living an unstructured life to living a very structured one. He would not be able to survive in his new environment unless he accepted the values of the new corporate entity of which he had become a part.

Leaders, as well as Followers, Must Commit to the Corporate Values

Leaders are not exempt from the need to adhere to the community's values as their own personal values. Leaders are a part of the corporate entity, but they aren't the entity itself. They are not above being governed by the community's values—although some leaders act as if they were. A leader should never tell a follower, "Do what I say—not what I do." He has a responsibility and an accountability to his followers, and he must demonstrate that he personally holds to the values of the group.

4. When There Is a Breakdown of Shared Core Values, Some Members Will Function According to Unspoken Negative Values

In organizations where positive values are not communicated, repeated, or demonstrated by the leaders, negative values can develop among the members as a means of personal survival and/or advancement. Individuals may start seeking a competitive advantage, rather than using their gifts for the benefit of the whole community.

Negative values are rarely talked about among the members of a corporate entity, except on the sly. These values may be in direct conflict with the organization's policies. Here are some commonly heard phrases in which people communicate, especially to new employees, the unspoken values of a company, as opposed to the formal ones:

+ "Don't contradict the boss."
+ "Never be the bearer of bad news."
+ "Anyone lower on the ladder is inferior."
+ "Don't rock the boat."
+ "Everyone is on the take."
+ "'Borrow' ideas and resources from other groups whenever possible."
+ "Always cover your butt."
+ "Win at all costs."

The message is that if you want to succeed in this organization, these are the things you should do and should not do. New or different ideas are not welcome. Many companies have an "underground" culture that can have an immediate negative effect on the values of new employees. These are some realities of the workplace that many people have to deal with.

How Negative Values Develop

Sometimes, negative values develop in an organization when members become frustrated by its practices and procedures. For example, they may find it difficult or impossible to make their required contribution to the group, due to flawed policies or a lack of cooperation from other members. Suppose a business had a policy that an employee was to complete a particular task through a certain department alone. The employee discovers that the members of that department won't work with him. So, he decides to work through someone else, in a different department, who has agreed to help him.

This way of functioning becomes a pattern for the employee. He has a difficult problem, yet he is establishing a negative value by ignoring the company's policy—one that had originally been set up to create an efficient process. Similar scenarios are found in businesses across the globe.

As a result, that employee may tell a new employee, "If you need something done, talk to so-and-so rather than going through the designated department," or, "Don't go by the book—do your job this way, instead."

Negative values can also surface when members reject a corporate value due to selfish reasons. For example, they may discard the value of competence and instead cut corners in order to get a job done faster, in hopes of obtaining praise from a supervisor. Or, they may discard the value of competence because they have become lazy and no longer have a passion to pursue excellence.

Many companies have an "underground" culture that can have an immediate negative effect on the values of new employees.

From Negative to Positive Values

Leaders of corporate endeavors need to become aware of unspoken negative values among their followers. They must discover why these unspoken values developed, and then help followers to recommit to, and realign with, the stated core values. Leaders should ask themselves questions such as the following: "Have I demonstrated the corporate values by my words and actions? Or have I exhibited a double standard?" "Do any corporate policies need to be updated in order to better align with our values and/or to help the group function better?" "Have I listened to what the members have been telling me about their difficulties in fulfilling their part of the corporate mission? What can I do to help them?"

Members must also recognize unspoken negative values in their community and assess whether they have accepted any of them. They should ask themselves questions such as the following: "Am I aligned with the corporate values?" "Have I accepted an unspoken negative value in order to solve a problem, instead of addressing the problem directly?" "Have I disregarded a corporate value due to carelessness, or in order to pursue my own agenda?" "Do I review the corporate values on a regular basis?" In addition, if the unspoken negative values of a group involve unethical conduct, individual members must remain committed to function according to a positive value system and code of ethics, rejecting peer pressure to compromise.

Vital Roles of Corporate Leaders

I have received invitations from leaders across the globe to whom I've presented the principles contained in this book. They have asked me to come and speak to all the employees of their company, or to all the civil servants from every department of their government. They have organized large meetings so that those employees and government workers could learn the significance of character. When strong values are "caught" by the members of an organization, the organization will be transformed in numerous positive ways.

Yet, as many of today's leaders try to fix the problems in their families, organizations, businesses, communities, and nations, they often focus only on power, diplomacy, or manipulation—over their family members, employees, associates, economic systems, institutions, and so forth. There is a great need for principled leaders who can...

+ Create an environment that will help individuals to discover, develop, refine, and exercise their abilities—providing an opportunity for their gifts to be served on behalf of the community and others. Good leaders do not only employ others; they deploy them.

+ Build a diverse but unified team, where each person can contribute his unique strengths, and where each person's weaknesses are either strengthened or made irrelevant by the complementary strengths of others.

+ Promote and demonstrate strong values, morals, and ethics, which have been translated into operational and relational standards—how people in the group conduct themselves as they contribute their strengths, and how they treat other members of the community and their constituents/clients.

Have you personally accepted the core values of your corporate vision? Do you demonstrate those values in your life and through your policies? Have you clearly communicated those values to your followers? This is the ◆ commission of a leader of character.

7

The Origin of
Our Moral Conscience

"If we are to go forward, we must go back and rediscover these precious values—that all reality hinges on moral foundations and that all reality has spiritual control."[1]
—Martin Luther King Jr.

S uppose you put your house on the market, after having just remodeled several rooms—creating a master-bedroom suite with a walk-in closet and a spa-like bathroom; installing custom-made cabinets, marble countertops, and new appliances in the kitchen; and converting the basement into an enormous family room. These improvements enabled you to raise your asking price considerably.

However, also suppose that the foundation of your home hadn't been properly supported, so that it suddenly became severely cracked, causing the house to tilt; or, imagine that a sinkhole developed, so that your house slipped into a deep pit. Under those conditions, no one would want to buy it! You couldn't even live in it yourself. If the house couldn't be salvaged, your improvements to the interior would have been for nothing. In reality, a house is only as valuable as the strength of its foundation. And its foundation is only as strong as what it is built upon.

The Bedrock Beneath Character

A foundation anchors a house to the ground. Yet, that foundation will not be secure if it hasn't been built upon solid rock, giving the house stability. Similarly, the anchor of a boat won't keep the vessel from drifting out to sea if it is not embedded in rock. Jesus of Nazareth told the following parable, unfolding a scenario similar to the one we looked at above:

> I will show you what he is like who comes to me and hears my words and puts them into practice. He is like a man building a house, who dug down deep and laid the foundation on rock. When a flood came, the torrent struck that house but could not shake it, because it was well built. But the one who hears my words and does not put them into practice is like a man who built a house on the ground without a foundation. The moment the torrent struck that house, it collapsed and its destruction was complete.[2]

I wrote earlier that one of our greatest weaknesses as leaders is that our philosophical training about who we are as human beings—including our inherent purpose—has been severely deficient. We have accepted flawed philosophies perpetuated by our culture. These flawed philosophies were built on foundations that were not supported by "solid rock."

Since character is the foundation of leadership, ask yourself, "On what have I constructed the current foundation of my beliefs, convictions, values, morals, and ethical code?" While you may embrace positive beliefs and values, have you built them on bedrock that is durable enough to keep the foundation of your character from cracking, sinking, or being swept away? In this chapter, we will consider the bedrock that our moral foundation must be anchored to in order to give our character lasting stability.

A Permanent Internal Guide

As we discuss the bedrock underneath character, let us begin with an inborn resource we all have: the conscience. To me, the conscience is like "default mode" in a computer. When people are unsure of what to do in a given situation, they may consult their conscience for direction. Or, when they are about to engage in a certain action, their conscience may suddenly rise up within them, giving them the conviction that the action is morally wrong, and they should not do it.

The word *conscience* is defined as "the sense or consciousness of the moral goodness or blameworthiness of one's own conduct, intentions, or character together with a feeling of obligation to do right or be good." The conscience is a permanent internal guide for a leader. Our thoughts and decisions will be either confirmed or challenged by the requirements of our conscience. In our heart, or subconscious mind, we recognize where our motivations and behavior are aligned with our conscience and where they have veered from it.

The Conscience Manifests in Beliefs and Convictions

A principled leader will be led by his conscience. That is why great leaders have always made statements such as "I have to do this," or "Even if you kill me, I cannot do that." (Remember that leadership passion is a desire that is stronger than death.) These statements are declarations of conscience. The leaders' consciences were speaking, and they were listening to them and following them. We need to ask ourselves, "Have I been listening to my conscience, or have I been ignoring it?"

Only when our beliefs align with our conscience can they manifest in strong convictions. And, as we know, convictions are what create our values, which become our moral standards, our ethics, and our character. In the end, our outward behavior is the product of our inner conscience. Remember that character is who we are when no one else is watching.

The Conscience Is Not the Same as the Emotions

Other people may not be able to observe our actions at all times, but our conscience is always aware of what we are doing. Since it is that part of us that counsels us concerning moral issues, I often refer to it as our *moral conscience.*

The moral conscience doesn't have to do with "feelings," as believed by some people who confuse the conscience with various emotions they experience. They will often rely on their feelings when making decisions, although emotions can be undependable when weighing options. Rather, the conscience is about *conviction.* The definition above referred to the *conscience* as a "sense or consciousness." It is moral certainty about the rightness or wrongness of our thoughts or actions. Thus, the conscience is distinct from the emotions, although a sense of conviction can *lead to* various emotions. We must learn to distinguish between the two through a process of careful evaluation and personal experience.

In addition, a principled leader does not allow himself to be advised by the opinions of the "crowd" over the convictions of his own conscience. For example, a politician who follows his conscience would be willing to stick with his principles, even though it might mean losing an election. Many leaders today would rather follow the crowd. As a result, their character is compromised. They may have developed certain convictions, but their convictions are not based on ethical concerns. They are based on self-centered considerations such as those we looked at earlier—attaining a certain position, controlling others, gaining wealth, and so forth.

In such cases, these leaders have made a decision—consciously or subconsciously—that something else is more important than what their conscience is telling them. They make choices based on what feels good to them, or an aspiration to obtain something, or a desire for excitement. They make such choices because they don't stop to think, check with their conscience, and reflect on the probable consequences of their actions.

The conscience is that part of us that counsels us concerning moral issues.

Ignoring the Conscience

Just as most leadership training today does not instruct people about character, it does not train people to follow their conscience. That crucial part of the human makeup is all but ignored. So, we produce leaders today who are not taught to value their conscience and to listen to it. Because of society's confusion about values and the nature of the conscience, many people have a conscience that has become underactive. We must all train ourselves to listen to our conscience. Those who do so will safeguard themselves from making wrong choices that would hurt them and/or others.

A leader who actively ignores his conscience will reap serious consequences for himself and his followers. We can ignore our conscience to the point that it becomes dull. It is even possible to develop a "seared" conscience—one that has been disregarded and denied for so long that it has essentially been silenced. For example, this may be what occurs in the lives of those who run financial scams for decades, even though they know the devastation they are wreaking on their clients' retirement funds.

Sometimes, we may wonder how people can commit acts that are outright evil. I believe the reason Adolf Hitler could have authorized the deaths of more than 10 million people in the Holocaust is that he ignored his conscience and chose to follow a contaminated philosophy. I don't believe anyone could order the extermination of multitudes of people and not have his conscience rise up at some point. To do such things, you have to ignore your conscience, not allow it to speak, and eventually "sear" it, so that you no longer hear it.

What Is Our "True North"?

Our moral conscience is like a compass. But it has a "true north" that evaluates and confirms its accuracy so that we can be sure we are steering the right course. It is also the measure by which our thoughts and feelings should be assessed to see if they line up with moral convictions. This author identifies "true north" as God. And in this context, I am referring to the God of the Bible. It was He who gave us the conscience as an element of the divine part of our human makeup.

Consequently, a properly functioning conscience is in sync with correct moral code. Even when a person has little knowledge of God, he has the conscience as a built-in regulator, telling him, "This is wrong," or "This is right," or "This is beneficial," or "This is not acceptable." I've talked with some people who claimed that the immoral actions they were involved in were perfectly acceptable. Yet if their conscience was still awake, they were not being honest with themselves or with me. They had a specific motivation for wanting to engage in that immoral conduct, but it was not based on their conscience. I would prefer to have someone admit to me that he's acting contrary to his conscience than to have him claim that his behavior is moral and try to convince me of that viewpoint, too. When he's honest with me about his actions, I can acknowledge where he's coming from, and we can be open with one another.

A Lost Understanding of True North

Many people no longer have an understanding about God, or they have purposely set aside that understanding. In the same speech from which the quote at the beginning of this chapter is taken, Martin Luther King Jr. suggested that Americans had "unconsciously left God behind." They had become involved in enjoying new technologies and an abundance of material goods, and, without meaning to, they had let their knowledge of the Creator, and their interest in Him, slip from their conscious thoughts.

I believe the same is true for many people in the world today. Yet a knowledge of God and His nature is the only "rock" on which we can secure the foundation of character. This knowledge must be restored to individuals and to nations. To help us to live according to His nature, God created us with a moral compass—the conscience. Yet He also gave us additional safeguards and guides for living: His precepts, or principles.

The word *principle* may be defined as "a comprehensive and fundamental law, doctrine, or assumption," "a rule or code of conduct," and "a primary source." The Creator gave us specific principles to follow that would establish our character in keeping with His, help us to better understand His nature and align with His purposes, guide our relationship with Him and other people, and enable us to be successful in fulfilling our inherent purpose.

Previously, we talked about how principles are crucial to our leadership success—how we all need to establish moral standards by which we will live our lives. Just as our character requires a bedrock that will hold it secure, our personal standards and principles—through which our character develops—must be built on the bedrock of the standards and principles our Creator has given us.

The principles contained in the biblical record are time-tested, stable, and civically sound. They can secure true human development. They can enable us to rebuild our societies and nations on a foundation of sound values and ethics. We need spiritual bedrock as the anchor for our character so that, when the storms of life shake us, and the quakes of current events wrench against our convictions, we will remain strong and steadfast.

What are some basic truths about God that many people have forgotten? How can these truths become the bedrock for the development of our character? Let's explore some answers to these questions.

We need spiritual bedrock as the anchor for our character.

We Are the Image and Likeness of Our Creator

We read in the first book of Moses,

Then God said, "Let us make man in our image, in our likeness, and let them rule over the fish of the sea and the birds of the air, over the livestock, over all the earth, and over all the creatures that move along the ground." So God created man in his own image, in the image of God he created him; male and female he created them.[3]

The above passage was the Creator's first public statement about human beings. He essentially said, referring to Himself, "Let Us create a being called 'man' and give him Our character—Our nature and characteristics." In this case, the word "man" is a plural noun; it refers to the species called *man*—both men and women.

In the Hebrew—the original language in which this passage was written—the word for "image" is *selem*, or *tselem*. This term indicates "'statue; image; copy.'...The word...means 'image' in the sense of essential nature.... Human nature in its internal and external characteristics...."[4] The word also signifies "a representative figure."[5] Humanity's nature was designed to be an image of the Creator's own nature, or character. God breathed His own life into man: "The Lord God...breathed into [the man's] nostrils the breath of life, and the man became a living being."[6] Thus, the Creator gave human beings something of His own Spirit. All human beings are meant to be representatives of God.

The word "likeness" in the passage is translated from the Hebrew word *demut*. It has the sense of "the original after which a thing is patterned."[7] We were patterned after our Creator to manifest His character as we live and work on this earth.

Character Is the Creator's Intrinsic Nature

What "pattern" are we cut from? How are we to represent the nature of the Creator through our character? Let's look at several of God's character qualities as illustrations.

Always Consistent

The Creator stated, "I the LORD do not change."[8] He is consistent; He is always the same. God changes things and circumstances. He also works in people so they can be transformed and become more like Him. But He Himself never changes. Accordingly, once a leader has established his life on solid, time-tested principles, he should continue to grow in knowledge, in experience, and in maturity, but he should never alter his good character. This means that even though you are progressing in life and growing in the exercise of your gifts, your fundamental nature should remain the same.

For example, it shouldn't matter whether you have only ten dollars to your name or a net worth of ten million dollars—your values and moral standards shouldn't deteriorate just because you have wealth (or power, or status, and so forth). You should be able to say something like the following in regard to your own experience: "I didn't steal so-and-so's twenty dollars when he dropped his wallet next to my car, and I'm not going to embezzle twenty million dollars now that I have access to my company's pension funds. I won't compromise my integrity."

There are people who have known me in public life for more than thirty years, and the greatest compliment some of them have given me goes something like this: "What I like about you is that you're still the same person. You have the same foundational beliefs, and you're saying the same things." I'd rather hear that said about me than anything else. Of course, I have grown personally, and I have developed professionally. But what these people are really telling me is that I have character. They are saying that I have been consistent; that, over the years, I haven't changed the essence of who I am. That means a lot to me.

Change is, of course, an inevitable part of our lives. In fact, I wrote a book on the topic of change several years ago because I believe we must learn how to respond positively to it and use it to our benefit as we fulfill our purpose in life. Yet, I emphasized that, amid all the changes in our lives, the Creator is our one constant. There are certain things that cannot be changed—the character of God and the principles He established for us to live by. Therefore, we can—and we must—grow. But we should not change our character.

Amid all the changes in our lives, the Creator is our one constant.

Always Predictable

Because the Creator's nature does not change, He is not one thing one day and another thing the next. He is predictable—in the best sense of the word. You know you can rely on Him. James, a first-century biblical writer, provided a fitting analogy for God's constancy when he wrote, "Every good and perfect gift is from above, coming down from the Father of the heavenly lights, who does not change like shifting shadows."[9]

In contrast, someone who is unpredictable about fulfilling his responsibilities is like "shifting shadows." He will confuse and inconvenience people—and he will often let them down in significant ways. To illustrate, suppose you had arranged with a family member to pick up your seven-year-old daughter from the school bus stop each day at 3:30 p.m. and stay with her at your house until you arrived home from work at 5:45 p.m. If your relative were unpredictable, she might decide on a whim one afternoon that she would skip picking up your daughter so she could go shopping, instead—without making alternate arrangements. She would cause your daughter to panic when no one came for her. You would become frantic about your child's safety when you arrived home and discovered that your daughter wasn't there, and that your family member—whom you reached on her cell phone at the mall—had no idea where she was. Your daughter might have wandered off and become lost or hurt—or worse. There also might be legal ramifications of child endangerment. Consistency—on many levels—is an essential character quality for meeting our responsibilities and maintaining good relationships with others, and it is an attribute that we are to model after our Creator.

Always Trustworthy

God's consistency and predictability make Him trustworthy. If you're not sure what someone is going to do, especially in regard to his conduct toward you, it's difficult to trust him. But when someone has consistently demonstrated his good character in the past, it is easy to trust him.

In the Bible, when God interacted with a person, He would often bring up His faithful relationships with those who had lived in previous generations, or His past acts of power on behalf of His people, in order to assure the individual of His present power and trustworthiness. For example, He made statements such as these: "I am the God of your father, the God of Abraham, the God of Isaac and the God of Jacob"[10]; "I am the LORD, who has made all things, who alone stretched out the heavens, who spread out the earth by myself"[11]; "I am the LORD who brought you up out of Egypt to be your God...."[12] With this evidence, He would attest to His absolute dependability.

We are to pattern our own behavior after the Creator's trustworthiness. When an employer asks a prospective employee for references, what he is really asking for are the names of reputable individuals who can provide a record of the applicant's competence and trustworthiness. He wants specific examples of how the applicant has demonstrated those qualities in his previous jobs or other life experiences.

Therefore, from time to time, we should ask ourselves, "How good are my 'references' regarding my trustworthiness? Would I receive good recommendations from my family, my friends, my neighbors, my coworkers, the members of my local community, the financial institution that holds the mortgage on my home, and so forth? In what areas of my life do I need to work on trustworthiness?"

Always Just

The Scriptures say, "The LORD is known by his justice."[13] Are you known for the same? Do you treat other people with impartiality, regardless of how they may treat you? Do you seek justice for those in your community? Let's look at a few of the instructions the Creator has given us in regard to justice—instructions that apply to both everyday interactions and legal matters:

> Do not spread false reports. Do not help a wicked man by being a malicious witness. Do not follow the crowd in doing wrong. When you give testimony in a lawsuit, do not pervert justice by siding with the crowd, and do not show favoritism to a poor man in his lawsuit. If you come across your enemy's ox or donkey wandering off, be sure to take it back to him. If you see the donkey of someone who hates you fallen down under its load, do not leave it there; be sure you help him with it. Do not deny justice to your poor people in their lawsuits.[14]

To be "just" means to regard everyone in an impartial way, not showing favoritism—whether you are dealing with friend or foe. May we be known for our justice, just as the Creator is.

Always Loving and Compassionate

"God is love."[15] The qualities of love and compassion are also foundational to the Creator's character: "Because of the LORD's great love we are not consumed, for his compassions never fail. They are new every morning; great is [His] faithfulness."[16]

Many people like to alleviate the suffering of people in their own nation or other nations who have experienced a great tragedy. For example, if a charitable organization makes an appeal for finances to help the victims of an earthquake or another natural disaster, the response rate is often very high. Yet it is sometimes easier for us to help people we don't know than to show continual kindness and compassion to those we do know personally, especially after they have disappointed or failed us.

Consistency in overlooking the faults and forgiving the wrongs of our family members, friends, and associates is a challenge. We should be grateful that the Creator has an endless supply of compassion for us every day, and we should seek to emulate His qualities in our relationships with others.

Of course, this doesn't mean that we should assist someone else to hurt himself or others by enabling his destructive behavior or addiction. Nor does it mean we should pretend everything is fine when serious issues exist in a relationship. However, whatever circumstances we are in, and whatever issues need to be resolved, we can approach others with the same principle of love with which the Creator approaches us—a love that values their creation in His image and seeks what is best for them physically, mentally, emotionally, and spiritually.

The nature of God is the epitome of character. He manifests all of the positive qualities associated with virtue, all of the time. He is therefore our ultimate model of character. And because He is perfect in character, we can count on Him to always be consistent, predictable, trustworthy, just, loving, and compassionate toward us.

Character Preceded the Gift of Leadership

Let's return to the passage in the first book written by Moses that describes the creation of human beings, as we continue to explore the principles the Creator has established for us to live by. "Then God said, 'Let us make man in our image, in our likeness....'" Note that the first thing on the Creator's mind regarding humanity was to give men and women character, or the essence of His nature. Clearly, character is His priority. And, as we have seen, it must be our priority, too, if we are to become the leaders we were meant to be.

The Creator's next statement was, "And let them rule...." Another way of translating "rule" is "have dominion."[17] In other words, He was saying, "Let them have leadership—authority and power—over the earth." Since character was God's priority, He gave the gift of His image and likeness *before* He gave the ability to rule. Significantly, He didn't consider it wise to entrust human beings with power until He had given them character.

We often do the opposite with our leaders—give people power and then *hope* they have character. If they don't, the way they use their power will expose that fact. But, from the start, character has always been imperative for human beings. And it should be the prerequisite for leaders today.

The Creator didn't entrust us with power until He gave us character.

Leadership Is Natural

The word "rule," or "have dominion," means to govern, to control, to manage, and to master. Because human beings received the gift of leadership in creation, it was natural to them. We were designed to rule and influence the earth according to God's character. That is why I wrote earlier that we were all born to lead in an area of gifting. We must grow into the leaders we were meant to be, by acknowledging and refining our leadership gifts and by developing character.

Many people are frustrated because they don't have a sense of purpose about why they are on this earth. Man's greatest ignorance is of himself. We have often disregarded or forgotten the reality of God and His purposes, as well as our having been created in His image and what it signifies. And, as we've seen, what we believe about ourselves creates our world. No human being can live beyond the limits of his beliefs. Having a knowledge of the Creator and what He designed us to be will give us a renewed sense of purpose.

Leadership Is a Cooperative Endeavor

Note that the Creator specifically stated, "Let *them* rule...." He didn't say, "Let *some* of them rule," or "Let *the elite* rule." Instead, He said, in effect, "Let *all* human beings rule." Dominion, or leadership, was established by God as a cooperative endeavor—and having character is essential for cooperating effectively with others.

The unique gifts we possess relate to the general human mandate to rule and to our individual fulfillment of that mandate alike. A community of leaders, each contributing his gifts and skills, is necessary to accomplish the overall leadership commission. God did not create the human race as a community that would have *a* leader or *some* leaders—He created a community *of* leaders. The idea that some people are superior and others are inferior doesn't exist in His plan.

Leadership Does Not Mean Dominating Other People

God said, "And let them rule over the fish of the sea and the birds of the air, over the livestock, over all the earth, and over all the creatures that move along the ground."[18] This list of areas over which human beings are to rule is especially instructive with respect to what's *not* included on it—*other human beings.* You and I were not meant to dominate other people, nor were we designed to be dominated by them. We were intended to exercise leadership over the earth's environment, animals, resources, physical properties, and so forth—but never other human beings. Again, dominating other people is illegitimate under the Creator's established purposes. That is why the human spirit naturally resists being controlled.

We Must Develop an Environment of Character

One of God's first instructions to human beings was, "Be fruitful and increase in number; fill the earth and subdue it."[19] The whole world was to be filled with men, women, and children who manifested the nature of God. Accordingly, we should develop an environment conducive to demonstrating God's character. Internally, we should develop the mind-set and qualities of character. Externally, we should create a community environment that promotes and upholds ethical standards, such as integrity and justice.

While there is no such thing as an "ethical community," there is such a thing as a community of ethical people. Corporately, the people agree on the values by which they are going to live. That agreement is what creates a culture of morality. And that moral culture becomes the source of ethics for the community. As we have seen, an ethical culture always begins with individuals' personal commitment to live according to strong values.

A Human Priority

The order the Creator set for leadership is *character before power.* That is why an emphasis on character must become a human priority again.

When we return to character, we return to the natural state in which we were meant to function.

You may be a manager, a supervisor, an entrepreneur, a politician, a clergyperson, an educational director, the chairperson of a community group, or the president of a nation. Whatever form of leadership you exercise, I urge you to make the following lifelong commitment: to help bring back character as the priority among leaders. Otherwise, our world will continue to spiral apart, morally and ethically. Across the globe, societies are deteriorating, and they will crumble if we don't make character our first concern.

The whole world was to be filled with men, women, and children who manifested the nature of God.

How Human Beings Lost Character

As we have discussed, a basic quality of the Creator's nature is that it doesn't change. The questions we must therefore ask are: "How did human beings as a race—made in God's image and likeness—lose the continual manifestation of His character?" "When did we stop being always consistent, always predictable, always trustworthy, always just, always merciful and compassionate, and so forth, as the Creator is?" "Why did we start to demonstrate unethical characteristics, so that our world has veered so far away from being an expression of His nature?"

Ironically, human beings lost their ability to consistently manifest the Creator's nature because the first man and woman heeded the false accusation that God wasn't treating them with true character—that He was not being just. When His trustworthiness was called into question, the first humans made a decision to doubt His authenticity. Then, for the sake of gaining power for themselves, they broke a key principle He had established for them. You can read about these incidents in the first book of Moses.[20]

The principle that the first human beings violated had been designed to protect them, so that they would not suffer the consequences of living outside of God's nature. In breaking this principle, they went against the very means that would have safeguarded them. Because they *chose* to live outside of God's nature, their character became warped. This indicates that, in some way, their character did not depend on nature alone—it also required an ongoing decision to remain in that nature. Today, we face the same type of decision: Will we live by our established principles, beliefs, values, moral standards, and ethical code? This is a choice we make on a daily basis.

The first humans' tragic decision caused humanity to suffer the consequences of a loss of God's true nature—including the onset of strife, sickness, and physical death. The fundamental source of all of humanity's deficiencies and problems was—and is—its rejection of the Creator's principles. This rejection is what the Scriptures call "sin." It is why human nature is described by spiritual leaders as being "fallen." It once existed on a high ethical plane, but it descended into a place where it often manifests only a fraction of its former state.

Results of the Loss of True Character

Let's explore several results of humanity's rejection of the principles and character of God.

1. Distortion of the Creator's Image

Because humanity lost God's true nature, it now has only a distorted image of that nature. The principal traits of fallen human beings are the opposite of genuine character: inconsistency, unpredictability, unfaithfulness, compromise, unjustness, prejudice, untrustworthiness, domination, vindictiveness, unforgiveness, cruelty, and so forth. All societies of the world suffer the symptoms of humanity's loss of character.

For example, there are people who connive to discredit their colleagues and other people in the workplace in order to get the promotions that these other individuals deserve. There are university students who cheat on tests in order to "achieve" a higher academic standing, with the result that they sometimes receive unfair advantages over others, such as higher-paying jobs. We wonder how these things can happen. (Some people aren't sure themselves why they commit some of these acts.) Moreover, humanity's warped character can cause the consciences of some people to be off-balance—they may lack a natural sense of guilt when doing wrong; or, they may have an overactive conscience, in which they continually feel guilty about things for which they are not responsible.

So, all human corruption stems from our loss of God's character as an intrinsic element of our own nature. Human beings are still capable of exercising moral conduct, but it involves making the continual decision to embrace strong convictions and values. And we are all inconsistent in this endeavor, because sound character is no longer natural to us.

2. Confusion About Self-image and Self-worth

Another result of human beings' rejection of God's image is that they lost their own essence. They became confused about who they were, what they were born to be, and how they were to live. They no longer had a clear sense of purpose and meaning in the world. And they forfeited the feeling of acceptance and worth that comes from being in unbroken relationship with their Creator.

3. Instability

Without character, human beings also became unstable. This is why it is often hard for us to depend on others. Many people neglect to keep their promises. For example, on their wedding day, a couple gets dressed up, stands in front of a clergyperson or a justice of the peace, and makes promises such as, "I will love and cherish you until I die!" Then, at some point after the honeymoon, the husband or wife may lose interest and leave—sometimes to run off with someone else. If your spouse has left you, you understand what I mean. You had a beautiful wedding in which everything was picture-perfect: the preacher, the gorgeous bridal gown and tailored tuxedo, the flowers, the rings, and more. It was an ideal day. And now you are wondering what happened to the marriage. Such heartbreak occurs because many people are unstable and inconsistent. They haven't made the conscious decision to establish strong values and truly commit to them.

If someone is unstable, it doesn't matter what he promises; you can't trust it. As the biblical writer James said, "Can both fresh water and salt water flow from the same spring? My brothers, can a fig tree bear olives, or a grapevine bear figs? Neither can a salt spring produce fresh water."[21] If the source hasn't changed, the result will be the same. James also wrote, "He who doubts is like a wave of the sea, blown and tossed by the wind.... He is a double-minded man, unstable in all he does."[22] An unstable person is like the waves of the sea—unpredictable, changeable.

That is why, when we meet people who have strong character, we admire and love them. It is because they are a picture of our original self. A person of character gives us a glimpse of what all human beings used to be like and what most of us, deep down, desire to be like. It is my hope that this book will reintroduce us to ourselves, will reconnect us to the image in which we were created. We were made for character, but we've been living outside of it. Let us become inspired to return to our true self—the image of God.

A person of character gives us a glimpse of what all human beings used to be like and what most of us, deep down, desire to be like.

The Restoration of Character

Because the Creator has genuine character, His plans for human beings did not include allowing them to languish in a state in which they lacked His nature—and experienced all the resulting consequences. In His faithfulness and trustworthiness, He initiated a plan to restore humanity to Himself. This plan involved giving us a renewed nature, one by which we would again be able to share His character and consistently follow His life-giving principles.

He accomplished this plan through Jesus of Nazareth, also called Jesus the Christ. God testified about Him, "This is my Son, whom I love; with him I am well pleased."[23] Jesus said, "I and the Father are one."[24] Jesus was God's Son because He came from God, He was one with God, and He fully manifested God's character on earth. One of Jesus' disciples wrote about Him:

In the beginning was the Word, and the Word was with God, and the Word was God. He was with God in the beginning. Through him all things were made; without him nothing was made that has been made. In him was life, and that life was the light of men.... The Word became flesh and made his dwelling among us. We have seen his glory, the glory of the One and Only, who came from the Father, full of grace and truth.[25]

And Paul of Tarsus wrote, "For in Christ all the fullness of the Deity lives in bodily form."[26] Jesus had the same nature and Spirit as God. And His purpose for coming to the earth was to restore the image of God in us. The Scriptures are very clear that we need a new nature. "No one can enter the kingdom of God unless he is born of water and the Spirit."[27] ♦

Therefore, Jesus came to give us back our character. No one can be restored to the Creator's nature except through Him.[28] Jesus the Christ, as the Son of God, was the only One who could represent both the Creator and His created beings in order to fix the breach between the two and bring about full reconciliation and restoration.

When Jesus Christ died on the cross, He paid the price for our fallen human nature. He also paid the price for all the times when we ourselves have acted contrary to the character and principles of our Creator. When we acknowledge and accept what He did for us, we are restored to God and receive His nature within us once again. This enables us to experience a lasting transformation by which we can manifest His image and develop genuine character according to His principles. In this life, we can expect to experience a process of ongoing growth and maturation in the way we manifest the Creator's nature.

Restoring a Culture of Character on Earth

God's "Kingdom"

When Jesus Christ was on earth, He emphasized the topic of the "kingdom of God" as He taught His disciples and the crowds who gathered to hear Him. I wrote earlier that the kingdom of God—the influence of heaven on earth—was Jesus' greatest value and priority. Let's look briefly at what the kingdom of God signifies.

God exists in a heavenly "country." He created earth to be like a colony of heaven, an extension of His kingdom. Such a culture could be produced only through beings who were like Him. As we have seen, He gave men and women the gift of leadership, or dominion, on the basis of their manifestation of His character. Yet when humanity rejected God's nature and principles, the full manifestation of His character on earth was lost.

Jesus made declarations such as, "The kingdom of God is near. Repent and believe the good news!"[29] He was referring to the return of God's culture to earth, which was inaugurated with His arrival and would be accomplished when He made provision for people to be restored to their Creator and receive the fullness of His nature once again.

The manifestation of God's nature on earth is called a "kingdom" because it is the realm over which He governs. It includes the community of all who have been infused with His nature as a result of their restoration to Him, so they can reflect His attributes. The renewal of God's culture on earth is the continuation of His original plan in creation—that the whole world would be filled with His character.

A Clash of Cultures

The word "repent," which Jesus used in announcing that the kingdom of God was near, has become a religious term, but it essentially means to change one's manner of thinking. For what reason did Jesus say people needed to alter their thinking? Because He was bringing back a different culture to the earth, and to be a part of that different culture required a different mind-set and different values.

This re-arrival of the kingdom of God on earth immediately brought about a clash of ideas and cultures. One reason is that the concepts of life that were advanced by the Roman Empire, including the idea that some races were superior to other races, dominated the world in which Jesus lived. And what Jesus taught was the opposite of the Roman outlook.

A Different Type of Leader

One of Jesus' most powerful statements about leadership is one in which He gave a commentary about Caesar and the Roman Empire:

> You know that the rulers of the Gentiles [the Roman leaders] lord it over them, and their high officials exercise authority over them. Not so with you. Instead, whoever wants to become great among you must be your servant, and whoever wants to be first must be your slave—just as the Son of Man did not come to be served, but to serve, and to give his life as a ransom for many.[30]

The standard behavior for leaders at that time was to control and manipulate other people, to throw around power and authority, and to tell others what to do. (Not much has changed, has it?) But Jesus told His disciples, in effect, "That's not the way it will be among you in God's kingdom. Your leadership will be different." What a distinction between the leadership perspectives of each culture! The first says, "To be great, you have to order other people around and show them who's the boss." The second says, "If you want to be great, if you want to be first, then you must serve other people." Jesus told His disciples, in effect, "Look at Me—I didn't come to be served. I came to give Myself." This point is crucial. What did Jesus give? Himself. True leadership means finding something within yourself to give.

The culture of the kingdom of God changes our conception of what it means to be a leader. Sometimes, we think that leadership is measured by how many people serve us, how many followers we have, or how many people are in our "entourage." I'm usually suspicious of people who have big entourages, because it suggests that they have an ego problem or a self-image issue. Leadership is not measured by how many people serve you. It's measured by whether you are serving other people.

And when you're serving other people, you're thinking about their value—that is what motivates and governs your relationship with them. When the Creator made us in His image, He established the value of all human beings. Sadly, wherever there is an absence of character, people find it easy to devalue others. But those who don't want to honor and serve people cannot be true leaders.

Leadership is not measured by how many people serve you. It's measured by whether you are serving other people.

Higher Standards *

Wherever the kingdom of God manifests on earth, therefore, it inevitably comes into ethical conflict with the prevailing culture. "Colonization" will lead to such dissonance, because one culture is entering another culture to replace it, not coexist with it. The culture of God's nature does not correspond with the destructive ideas that have developed from fallen human nature, and such ideas are dominating our nations today. It will take principled leaders to bring about transformation—and not merely become absorbed into the existing system.

We can no longer function according to the false patterns of leadership we see exhibited in our culture. I know that many of us were trained according to traditional concepts of leadership, such as the Roman Empire promoted; many of us received our degrees from schools that taught these ideas. Yet our standards must be higher.

Although you may experience "cultural clashes" as you begin to live by the Creator's principles, don't let those encounters cause you to respond in anger toward other people. True leaders serve; they don't push other people around.

For example, in the last chapter, we talked about how unspoken negative values can dominate a corporate entity. People may tell a new employee such things as, "Look, if you're going to be a part of this company, you have to do what everyone else is doing. Otherwise, you have to leave." What they're insinuating is, "We've got a certain culture in this organization, and everybody's on the take. So, if you don't try to get your piece of the pie, then you are going to be a problem for us because you will expose us. Either you become part of the group, or you won't survive."

In such a situation, a leader must remain steady—dedicated to the values, principles, and ethics by which he has committed to live. Cultures will be transformed as we follow our moral conscience, consistently manifest the qualities of God's nature, and seek to serve others.

8

The Power of Principles

When a consumer product is developed and produced, its manufacturer often publishes important information about it in a user's manual that is packaged with the item. The manual is actually a book of "principles" indicating how the item functions, how to properly operate it, and how to make it last longer. Some of these principles might be: "Keep away from heat." "Always clean appliance after using." "Do not use near or place in water." "Not intended to bear weight exceeding 10 pounds." "Observe recommended maintenance schedule."

Similarly, after creating the first human beings, the "Manufacturer" gave them valuable information about how they "functioned," how to properly "operate" their lives, and how to ensure that their leadership would have longevity. He conveyed specific principles so they could understand the nature by which they had been designed to live. Later on in human history, He made sure these principles, and additional instructions, were put into writing as a vital reference for all of humanity.

Earlier, we discussed the fact that the values of an organization or community should always be conveyed clearly to its members. And we are all members of the largest community on earth—the human race. The Creator has "published" His principles and values in various ways in the Bible, which is, in effect, a "Corporate User's Manual" for human beings. Some of these principles and values are included in compilations of moral standards, two of which are commonly known as the Ten Commandments and the Beatitudes. But many more may be discovered in its pages—some of which we explored in the previous chapter.

In chapter 7, I wrote that the principles contained in the biblical record are time-tested, stable, and civically sound. They can secure true human development and enable us to rebuild our societies and nations on a foundation of sound values and ethics. In addition, if an individual who has suppressed his conscience, or moral compass, becomes aware of the Creator's principles, and responds to them, his conscience can be reawakened, so that he will regain a conviction of right and wrong. For all these reasons, I have designed this chapter as an overview of the key properties and benefits of the principles the Creator has established for us.

The Key to Leading Effectively

The power of principles has been among the greatest discoveries of my life, and I believe the same can be true for you. The key to living effectively on this earth is to know, accept, and apply the Manufacturer's principles. Comprehending these principles will give us wisdom, and following them will make us leaders of character.

The Manufacturer—Not the Product— Sets the Principles

The first key property to understand about principles is that a manufactured product does not establish the principles by which it functions— the creator/manufacturer does. As we have noted, everything our Creator/ Manufacturer made was designed to operate according to principles He had determined in advance. That includes us human beings. So, the principles by which we function have already been defined by our Creator; they are not defined by us.

The Purpose of Principles

These principles are not arbitrary but are specific to our purpose: We were meant to operate according to principles that can uphold our moral nature in God's image and likeness. Therefore, it is in our best interest to understand and follow them.

"First Laws"

We have previously defined a *principle* as "a comprehensive and fundamental law, doctrine, or assumption," "a rule or code of conduct," and "a primary source." The word *principle* is derived from two Latin words meaning "beginning" and "initiator." Accordingly, principles refer to "first laws."

The Creator's "first laws" for life on earth pertain to both the physical and the moral (spiritual) realms. God instituted physical laws, such as the force of gravity, to govern our earthly environment, giving us the parameters for how we may function in the natural world. Likewise, He instituted moral laws for the conduct of our lives, giving us parameters for how we may live in an ethical way with respect to Him, ourselves, and other people.

Comprehending principles will make us wise, and following them will make us leaders of character.

Principles Are Permanent

Another key property of God's principles is that they are unchanging, or permanent. We can resist them, but that does not alter them or the consequences of rejecting them. To use a familiar example, you could try to defy the law of gravity by jumping off a building, believing that you would float down to safety, simply by wanting it to happen. Yet gravity would still pull you down to the ground—in effect, saying, "I'm going to prove to you that physics works!" Fixed laws apply to everyone.

All of life relates to physical and/or moral principles. We are concerned in this book with exploring moral principles, which lead to character, as well as the consequences of disregarding them. Therefore, let's look at some benefits of learning, and adhering to, the Creator's eternal principles.

Benefits of Knowing and Following the Creator's Principles

Principles Safeguard Us from Substitutes

Principles enable us to build and maintain personal character as they govern and safeguard our lives. While the "first laws" are those the Manufacturer instituted and stated in His User's Manual, there are other moral laws we must view with caution because they are substitutes for the originals. These were invented by some of the Manufacturer's "products."

For example, many people today are advancing their own principles regarding what conduct is morally and ethically acceptable. The reason many of our nations are experiencing decline is that they are being led by influential people whose philosophies are based on other "manuals." These cultural leaders claim that the revised principles are better than the ones the Manufacturer established. Yet the new principles are not recognized by the Manufacturer and will not lead to lasting success, according to the laws He has established for the world. We cannot institute "new" natural laws. And we cannot alter the inherent principles by which human beings have been created to function.

Perhaps you've had the experience of preparing for a week-long trip and trying to decide what to pack. In such a situation, many people tend to overpack, so they have to sit on top of their suitcase in an attempt to shut it. The suitcase's sides bulge, and its zipper becomes strained. Often, after several unsuccessful attempts, people end up taking out some of their items because the case wasn't designed to hold that much volume. Sometimes, however, people succeed in shutting the lid, and then they have to lug around a heavy suitcase. If they're traveling by plane, they may have to pay an extra fee due to the extra weight of their luggage. Then, by the time they return home, the seams of the suitcase have started to pull apart, and the fabric is fraying.

This scenario is similar to what happens when we try to add "new" principles that don't fit in with the Creator's original design—they become burdensome and damaging to us. Some people claim that shifting morals indicate social progress—leading the way for human development and reengineering. However, they fail to recognize the consequences to human development of tampering with, or rejecting, integral principles. Such new laws may garner popular support, but they won't cancel first laws, which, again, are as fixed, morally speaking, as physical laws are.

Here's another simple illustration. Suppose an individual decided he wanted to forgo using gasoline to run his car, so he filled his tank with orange juice, instead. He had the will to do this, and he had the ability to do it, but his action didn't alter the principle of how an internal combustion engine works. As originally designed, his car won't run unless he puts fuel in it. And putting orange juice in his tank will damage the engine.

In this regard, let's look at some statements found in the User's Manual, in the book called the "Psalms," in which the biblical writer is addressing the Creator:

> You have laid down precepts
> that are to be fully obeyed.[1]

The word "precepts" refers to first laws. The writer was saying, in effect, "Creator, You've laid down principles that are not optional; they are not open for discussion." Although they are permanent, first laws are not stagnant. On the contrary, they are applicable to all people, in all eras of history, and they are life-giving. Later on in the passage, we read,

> I will never forget your precepts,
> for by them you have preserved my life.[2]

Next, let's look at the opening lines of another psalm, written by King David, about leaders who try to function according to principles contrary to those the Creator has set:

> Why do the nations conspire
> and the peoples plot in vain?
> The kings of the earth take their stand
> and the rulers gather together
> against the LORD and against his Anointed One.
> "Let us break their chains," they say,
> "and throw off their fetters."[3]

The next part says,

The One enthroned in heaven laughs;
the Lord scoffs at them.[4]

Why does the Creator "laugh" at this conspiracy? Since His principles are already set, any plots against them are in vain. People are inventing their own laws, but they won't work. God has already determined the best way for us to function.

The Creator isn't impressed by any governmental leader or legislative body that creates laws contrary to the ones He has built into life. Neither is He threatened by them. He is our ultimate Leader, and His authority cannot be supplanted by those whom He has created.

Though we can't invent principles that will cancel the Manufacturer's first laws, that doesn't mean that people won't attempt to create them and live according to them. But if they do, they won't be living in harmony with themselves, with others, or with their Creator. They won't function as they were designed to.

Following God's established standards is the only way human beings can live productively and peacefully. Yet many people seem to fight against these principles. I believe that if they understood the essential purposes of God's first laws, they would stop fighting them and benefit from their life-giving power.

Principles Simplify Our Lives and Decision-Making

Another reason the Creator's principles are eminently valuable is that they simplify life. When you understand His principles, you know how to respond in a variety of situations—especially those that involve ethical questions. You must take time to learn God's laws, but when you do, they will make many of your decisions clearer and easier.

The first psalmist I quoted in the previous section also made this statement:

I will walk about in freedom,
for I have sought out your precepts.[5]

The writer was saying that because he had "sought out" the Creator's principles, he knew he would "walk about in freedom." When we follow God's first laws, we are liberated. We are, as we discussed, set free to make decisions about various issues and dilemmas without having to wonder what to do. And we are also free from the negative consequences that come from making poor ethical decisions. Thus, observing foundational principles enables us to walk with a new confidence.

Let's look at one more excerpt from the passage quoted above:

I have more insight than all my teachers,
    for I meditate on your statutes.
I have more understanding than the elders,
    for I obey your precepts.[6]

If you study the Creator's principles, you'll become much wiser than many leaders today. I frequently interact with powerful, influential people, and when I'm asked to present my ideas for solving certain societal or corporate issues, the leaders often comment on the wisdom contained in those ideas. What many of them don't realize—especially at first—is that I have studied many of God's integral principles. I can't take credit for the wisdom. As a consultant, my role is to explain and expound upon these principles to them. When they first hear the principles, they think they are new and remarkable. They are remarkable—but they are not new. Once more, they are long-established and time-tested.

If you study the Creator's principles,
you'll become much wiser than many leaders today.

Consequently, if someone is having a problem with his company, and he asks me to serve as a consultant to address the issue, I often know exactly what to advise right away, because most problems involve violations of first laws—principles of ethics, principles of right relationships, principles of sound financial practices, and so forth. At times, I can identify most problems within a company in a matter of hours. Why? I'm not looking at personalities or agendas—I'm looking for the key principles the leaders and their employees are ignoring or rejecting.

If you understand principles, therefore, discovering solutions to a variety of concerns will become second nature. To return to the automobile analogy, suppose the fuel gauge of your car was below "E." You wouldn't have to wonder what to do in order to get your car to continue to function. The decision would be simple, because you would know the "principle." Even if you didn't know much about engines, you would know the most important law to apply in order to make your car run again: Put some gas in it. Likewise, in the moral arena, you don't have to question how to respond when someone asks you to do something dishonest, reckless, vengeful, and so forth. When you know first laws, or principles, you know exactly what to do—and what not to do.

In the Corporate User's Manual, the book of Proverbs gives much practical wisdom that we can apply in a number of situations. One passage, using an illustration from the natural world, addresses the perils of laziness and the rewards of working to provide for your own needs:

> Go to the ant, you sluggard; consider its ways and be wise! It has no commander, no overseer or ruler, yet it stores its provisions in summer and gathers its food at harvest. How long will you lie there, you sluggard? When will you get up from your sleep? A little sleep, a little slumber, a little folding of the hands to rest—and poverty will come on you like a bandit and scarcity like an armed man.[7]

In another section of the User's Manual, Jesus of Nazareth discusses our need to address our own shortcomings before trying to correct others' faults:

> Why do you look at the speck of sawdust in your brother's eye and pay no attention to the plank in your own eye? How can you say to your brother, "Brother, let me take the speck out of your eye," when you yourself fail to see the plank in your own eye? You hypocrite, first take the plank out of your eye, and then you will see clearly to remove the speck from your brother's eye.[8]

Principles Enable Us to Fulfill Our Potential

Violating the Creator's principles will also prevent us from reaching our full potential. If we follow His laws, we can fulfill our destiny. If we don't, we will never reach it. For instance, the "destiny" of your car is to mobilize you and transport you safely to your destination. Yet, if you were to violate a key principle related to the vehicle—for example, if you were to continue operating the car after allowing the oil pan to run dry, so that you ruined the engine—you would have nullified the manufacturer's promises about its functioning. Similarly, the success of your future depends on your obedience to key principles established by your Manufacturer—the Creator.

Obedience is not a negative word. In this sense, to obey merely means to follow proven principles. Suppose you were to place grain seeds on a clean tile floor. When you came back after a few days, you would see that they had not sprouted or taken root. They need to be planted in soil to do that. So, every time you plant seeds in the ground, you are submitting to the principle of growth established by the Creator. Likewise, when you adhere to His moral principles, you are submitting to a vital standard for fulfilling your personal potential as a leader. Remember that character ensures the longevity of leadership, and men and women of principle will leave important legacies and be remembered by future generations.

As we saw earlier, the process of applying a principle requires that you must first know what the principle is (for example, you have to know that your car requires fuel to function). Second, you must value, or accept, the principle (you become convinced of the need to put fuel into your car). Third, you must act on the principle (by actually putting fuel into your car's gas tank). You would barely think about the process described in this illustration if you'd been around automobiles from the time you were a child, so that the process had become second nature. Nevertheless, each step is necessary, and we must realize that the process applies to the implementation of principles in many contexts.

Without First Laws, Life Is an Experiment

When people don't know or obey first laws, they begin to experiment with foundational elements of human life, including values and morals. These substitute laws are "experiments" because the people promoting them have little understanding of what is going to happen to individuals and society if the new laws are promoted and practiced. Experimentation is beneficial and necessary in relation to scientific inquiry, creative endeavors, and so forth. But experimentation in moral matters is a dangerous practice.

Experimentation Leads to Distrust and Disillusionment

The average leader in the world today has not been trained in the Manufacturer's principles, so he often has to make up his responses when confronted with societal issues and problems. This means that many of the leaders of your country are merely guessing about how to deal with national problems. So, your country's future is, in essence, an experiment for them. They keep trying this policy and that policy, but few of them work.

One outcome of society's experimentation with ethics has been people's growing distrust of authority, leading to their disillusionment. When leaders of all walks of life lack character and experiment with principles, their constituents don't have anyone they can really trust. By and large, in our society today, the younger generations don't trust the older generations, and the older generations don't trust the younger generations—or even themselves. Citizens don't have confidence in their politicians, and politicians don't have regard for the citizens. Parishioners don't respect their priests and ministers, and the priests and ministers don't esteem the parishioners. Likewise, students don't respect their teachers, and the teachers don't esteem their students.

This widespread distrust has resulted in varying degrees of apathy, compromise, permissiveness, sexual confusion, a devaluation of human life, and a culture of violence and death. Our experimentation must be replaced with the application of first laws in regard to the fundamental values of human life.

Experimentation in moral matters is a dangerous practice.

Experimentation Leads to Lawlessness

We have seen that, in the optimal scenario, a country's laws are based on values and standards by which the citizens in the national community have agreed to live. This is why a nation can reflect a national ethic. If the citizens value a certain standard, it becomes a law to them. If the individual citizens agree to abide by that law, they become moral. Their conduct, then, becomes ethical.

Yet this process has broken down today. Values and standards are often considered relative. People say things such as, "What's right for you isn't necessarily what's right for me. Therefore, you can't impose your standards on me." This viewpoint can apply only so far, because our world was designed with fixed principles and moral absolutes, without which a society can't function in a healthy way. And individuals must exercise personal responsibility in relation to these fixed principles and moral absolutes.

Experimentation in ethical issues results from not having—or acknowledging—moral references or parameters, so that nothing is "settled." Instead, relativism and license take over. License contrasts with the freedom that is gained from following sound principles; it leads to lawlessness, which is a rejection of natural laws and standards. I believe that a spirit of lawlessness has affected every level of society today.

The only way to solve lawlessness is to restore character. Principled leaders are those who establish moral boundaries and set ethical "stakes." We need people who will say, "This is what I believe," and "This is the boundary. This is where we stand."

Leaders who have not comprehended moral principles, or who have rejected them, have led us into lawlessness. It will take leaders who understand moral principles, who live by them, and who establish ethical policies to lead us back to lawfulness. Laws can help to create character as people adhere to them.

Many people say, "Governments cannot legislate morality." I believe the opposite. Let us not be fooled into believing that political decisions and policies are morally neutral. Why? Because all decisions have moral implications, and therefore all governmental policies and laws are "moral"—they reflect the values and ethics of those who institute them. You can't create a law that doesn't reflect a moral code. And codes regulate conduct. Yet, as we know, a society can be only as strong as the number of its members who value its laws and adhere to them personally.

Moral principles can be promoted in the context of any form of "government," not just political entities. Such standards can be set by all types of leaders, on all levels—whether leaders of a family, a civic group, a university, a business, a nation, or another entity. Implementing some form of rules, policies, or codes of acceptable behavior is what all "governments" do.

Experimentation Leads to Loss and Destruction

When leaders try to implement principles that they have fabricated, and that are in opposition to the Manufacturer's first laws, "malfunctions" will occur. To act in a way contrary to the User's Manual is to risk damage to the "product." Picture a lighthouse in a storm, with waves crashing high against it. The waves are in motion, but the lighthouse is stable; it is grounded. The principles given to us by the Creator are like lighthouses— they remain constant, and they provide light that guides us to solid ground.

To act in a way contrary to the Corporate User's Manual is to risk damage to the "product."

I was born in a very poor neighborhood in the Bahamas. My ten brothers and sisters and I slept on the floor of our two-bedroom wood house, the corners of which rested on four stones. In my neighborhood, questionable characters were always present, exerting a negative influence. But when I discovered the Creator's principles, they not only changed the way I thought about myself, but they altered the course of my life. I recognized the potential within me and gained a vision for my life that has stayed with me to this day.

A number of my fellow classmates had great potential. However, many of our teachers would tell the students, "You are a failure. You'll always be a failure, and nothing but a failure." After some time, a lot of the students would finally believe it, and say, "There's no use in trying. I'm just going to fail this exam, anyway, so I might as well not study." Sadly, many did fail in school and never fulfilled their potential.

Other classmates' lives went off track because they violated moral principles and laws. Some of them are in prison now. When I visit them, they say, "You've done well." I reply, "I've just made some decisions that were different, that's all."

Whether a person consciously or unconsciously violates first laws, the result is decline and destruction. Most things in life aren't killed; they die on their own. The Creator did not say to the first human beings, "If you disobey Me, I will kill you." He said, in effect, "If you disobey this first principle, you will certainly die."[9] He knew the inevitable consequences of violating bedrock principles.

Destruction from within—whether it is within an individual, a family, a business, a church, a volunteer organization, a local community, or a country—is a sign of either a lack of awareness of first laws, a rejection of them, or both. Similarly, no matter what kind of crime someone may commit—a misdemeanor, a white-collar crime, or a violent crime—it is the result of a denial of principles.

If a leader does not know first laws and implement them, I can predict the future of his organization. You may be a leader who has been ignoring time-honored principles. Perhaps, by using your charisma and exhibiting enthusiasm, you have gotten people excited about following you and your vision. But, underneath, your foundation is not secure.

Your organization may grow at first. Yet when it gets to a certain size, it will stop expanding, because you haven't applied the principles necessary for it to grow beyond that point. Corporate growth is not all about business plans, investments, and top-notch employees. You also have to conduct business honestly; make wise decisions; and hire people who have integrity, who have a passion for the corporate vision, and who value and support the contributions of all their coworkers.

Recommit to the Principles in the Corporate User's Manual

It doesn't make a difference what the current issues, trends, and fads may be—if you know and follow first laws, you will outlast temporal matters. Leaders of character do not live by transient movements or emotions but by solid principles. Again, emotions are part of the human makeup.

However, leaders of character are not guided by how they feel on a particular day; they are guided by the principles that form their lifelong convictions and values.

No matter what type of leadership you exercise, don't forget first laws! Perhaps you are a leader in a local, regional, or national government who is in a position to tackle contemporary problems and to help develop laws and civic programs. Or, maybe you are a leader in your business or organization who is in a position to develop corporate plans and to set policies. If you violate the Manufacturer's principles, you will contribute to the weakening of your nation, your company, or your organization.

Leaders of character are guided by the principles that form their lifelong convictions and values.

Recommitting to first laws is like rebooting a stalled computer by pushing the reset button—it allows us to return to the "original mode" where we can function as we were intended to. By studying and implementing the principles in the User's Manual, you will avoid moral compromise and ethical missteps. You will protect yourself from the negative effects that such mistakes inevitably have on other aspects of your life, including the exercise of your gifts and the realization of your potential. You will also gain much practical wisdom for leadership. You will be able to say, with the biblical writer, "I will walk about in freedom, for I have sought out your precepts."[10]

PART III:

Personal Character Development

9

Key Concepts of Character

"We manifest character when self-sacrifice for the sake of
our principles becomes more important to us than compromise
for the sake of popularity."
—Dr. Myles Munroe

This section of the book focuses on how we can actively engage in
personal character development. Let's set the stage by talking about
storytelling. In novels, screenplays, and other forms of fictional narratives,
there is an element called the "character arc." Usually, the hero starts out in
one situation, having a particular mind-set about his life. After progressing
through a series of events and challenges while attempting to reach a personal goal, he ends up in a new place in his life, with a changed perspective.
The "arc" refers to the protagonist's personal transformation as he journeys
from where he was at the beginning of the story to where he arrives at its
conclusion.

Following the Character Arc

For example, in the classic film *On the Waterfront*, the main character,
Terry, played by Marlin Brando, begins his character arc as a washed-up
boxer who is intimidated by the corrupt union boss he works for. The boss,
who has ties to the mob, exploits the longshoremen, and Terry is told to
put pressure on one of the men who is trying to expose his corruption.
Terry is shocked when the encounter leads to the man's death. Although
the incident deepens his low opinion of himself, Terry finds himself falling
in love with the sister of the dead man.

The union boss orders the murder of Terry's brother, who refused to kill Terry at the boss's order. At this point, the demoralized former boxer summons the courage to stand up to the boss in defense of the oppressed longshoremen. He proves his willingness to sacrifice for his newfound convictions when he is severely beaten up and almost killed. By the end of the story, completing the character arc, Terry has discovered a strength and resilience within himself that he never would have thought possible in his "old life." In the process of his trials, he becomes a leader among his peers and someone who has demonstrated true character.

Like the protagonist in a story, you, too, will experience a "character arc" as you develop and refine your moral standards and principles, so that you can be transformed personally and professionally. In fact, you will progress through many "character arcs," since the process of character development is ongoing. A novel or screenplay may cover only a small portion of a protagonist's life. The story may take place over a matter of days or weeks, and that period of the character's life is all we learn about him. However, in "real life," the hero would encounter a number of other challenges that would take place after the events of the story have ended.

In this chapter, we will look at several practical illustrations and key concepts of character that we have examined throughout this book. This will lead us to chapter 10, in which we will explore in greater depth the secret to successful character development.

Illustrations of Character

The English word *character* comes from a Latin word meaning "mark," or "distinctive quality." As we have seen, our character is what marks, defines, and identifies us. And we've been asking ourselves, "What distinctive qualities identify me? Are they positive or negative?" Genuine character includes the following features: It is (1) fixed, or set, (2) predictable, and (3) stable.

1. Character Is Fixed, or Set

Most people are familiar with the saying, "Every man has his price." This idea implies that every person has a point at which he will compromise his moral standards to gain something else that is a higher priority to him. Some of the usual candidates are money, fame, and power. But if we want to be leaders of character, we have to stop accepting this notion—right now. There's no "price" for a leader of character that will cause him to compromise his standards, because his principles are his life. All leaders of character are therefore "set in their ways," ethically speaking.

There's no "price" for a leader of character that will cause him to compromise his standards.

The fixed quality of character may be illustrated by elements whose intrinsic quality is to be unchanging, or absolute. For example, the letters of the alphabet within a particular language are fixed. (Each letter is also called a "character," in reference to being a "mark.") For instance, *A* is always *A*. It will never turn into *C*. The same property is true for all of the letters of the alphabet. The meanings of the individual letters do not change. If they were not set, the system of using them to communicate meaning among people who share a common language would fail. It would lead to mass confusion.

Moreover, a number of languages in the world share some or all of the basic Latin alphabet. For example, the French and Portuguese languages use the identical twenty-six letters of the alphabet that the English language does. The Spanish language adds only one letter. The pronunciation of the letters differs, but the fact that the alphabets are fundamentally equivalent simplifies the process of learning these related languages. Similarly, moral absolutes give people solid parameters that enable them to understand the world they live in and to interact with others in a meaningful way.

Numerals are another example of the fixed nature of character. The number 1 is always 1. It will never change to become 2. And so on, up to infinity. In nations across the globe, the properties and functions of numbers are used in exactly the same way.

An additional example of the set nature of character is that of physical laws. As we discussed in a previous chapter, the Creator's moral principles function in a parallel way to His physical laws, such as gravity—they are unchanging, and they apply to all of us.

Let's conclude this section by looking at a final illustration taken from the properties of a commonly used building material—cement. If cement is wet, it is malleable, enabling you to form a specific shape—often adding other materials to it first—using a mold. For instance, you might use it to make sections of a concrete sidewalk or concrete building blocks.

However, once cement hardens, or sets, you can't reshape it. If you want to make something different, you need to start with fresh cement. I heard a story about some cement workers who forgot to keep the drum of their large cement mixer rotating. By the time they realized their error, the cement in the drum had completely dried, and they knew there was nothing they could do to salvage it. The cement was now set and unchangeable. Those workers had to spend hours using sledge hammers to remove all the dried cement from the drum so it could be used again.

When cement is set—hopefully, as intended—you know that the sidewalk, concrete blocks, or whatever else you have formed will be solid and secure. Likewise, a person with character is "set" in the sense that he cannot be changed from holding to his established convictions and standards. Suppose someone offered you cash under the table to look the other way in an illegal business transaction, and said, "Just pretend you didn't see this. Let it go." If you agree to look the other way, your character is not "set." Your values are still malleable. But if you refuse, your character is solid and secure. That is why we must learn to exercise the kind of personal discipline that will say, "I cannot do this. It's against my convictions."

2. Character Is Predictable

In chapter 7, we discussed several attributes of the Creator, one of which is that He is always "predictable." To be predictable is to be consistently responsible and trustworthy. We can rely on God because He is not one thing one day and another thing the next.

Would you say that your conduct is predictable or unpredictable? For example, is your temperament consistent? Do your family members and coworkers have to walk around on tiptoe when they see you because they don't know how you will react to them on a given day? Do they have to warn others, "Watch out—he's in a bad mood today!" One biblical writer described Jesus of Nazareth as "the same yesterday and today and forever."[1] That is the way our character should be. Moreover, when we demonstrate that we are reliable, we give other people a sense of security and well-being.

A principled leader is predictable to the point that his character speaks for him in his absence. That is to say, people know him so well that they could vouch for what he would or would not do in a given situation—and be totally accurate. Consequently, as one gauge of how strong your character is, you might ask several people you trust to give you an honest assessment of what they think your conduct would be under various scenarios. Use that information to help you form and strengthen your character.

> *A principled leader is predictable to the point that his character speaks for him in his absence.*

3. Character Is Stable

As we noted earlier, one consequence of humanity's loss of true character was instability. The first-century writer James said that a double-minded man is unstable in everything that he does.[2] I think James was saying that if a person has a character defect in one area, he will inevitably have character flaws in other areas, as well. And it's hard to trust a person who keeps vacillating.

Instead, when we walk with integrity, our good character can flow evenly in all areas of our life. Jesus of Nazareth told a concise parable describing how the nature of the Creator is meant to fill us. He said that the kingdom of God is "like yeast that a woman took and mixed into a large amount of flour until it worked all through the dough."[3] Character must "work its way" through every part of us, so that we can consistently manifest it to others.

Another excellent illustration of the stability of character is that of a statue. Perhaps you have a favorite statue—the Statue of Liberty in New York Harbor; the "Christ the Redeemer" statue in Rio de Janeiro, Brazil;

Michelangelo's *David* in Florence, Italy; or a statue in your community. One of my favorite statues is of Queen Victoria, located in Parliament Square in downtown Nassau, Bahamas. The statue is carved completely of marble, and the famous queen is depicted as a young woman, sitting with a royal scepter and a sword, wearing a crown and flowing robes, and smiling serenely.

The statue was placed in the square in 1905, so I've never known a time when it wasn't there. Because it has remained unchanged for decades, it always reminds me of the stability and resilience of character. I see this statue frequently in my comings and goings, and no matter what the weather conditions, the statue does not appear altered. It could be a day when the temperature reaches 100 degrees Fahrenheit, and everyone in town is wilting from the heat, but "Victoria" continues to smile. During the rainy season, the downpours are so heavy at times that you can hardly see in front of you. The rain comes down like lead, and it beats on the statue, but she smiles through it all. That statue has also been through every hurricane in the Bahamas since the early twentieth century, including Hurricane Sandy in 2012. It has endured 140-mph winds, staying strong in the midst of the storms.

Moreover, someone might go up to "Queen Victoria" and insult her, but she would just keep smiling at the person and never retort. You could go to her in the middle of the day, and she would still be sitting and smiling. You could "sneak up" on her at two in the morning, and she'd be smiling. When no one is in Parliament Square looking up at her, she is still smiling. One time, I saw a bird land on her head and "relieve" itself on her—even then, she kept her serenity! I can guarantee what she is doing right now without being in her presence, because I know she is unchanging—she has "character."

Similarly, a principled leader does not change his values and principles, no matter the external circumstances. He is able to weather all kinds of personal and professional storms, even those that are "hurricane strength," while remaining calm and steadfast. We need to ask ourselves the following: "Am I consistent, no matter where I am, what I am doing, and what time of day it is?" "What do I do when people 'relieve themselves' on me—in other words, gossip about me, criticize me, attack my motivations, insult me, or even swear at me? Do I become a different person, losing my temper and lashing back?" "What would I be like if my business collapsed and I lost everything? Regardless of how devastated I felt, would my character remain the same?" "Am I the really the person that I project to others?" "Do I behave in an unethical or inappropriate way when no one else is around?"

A true leader is able to take criticism and mistreatment and still retain his character. Genuine character will outlast all disagreements, disapproval, opposition, and attacks. If you believe in your ideas and your standards, you should stay with them—be stable. Even your enemies may eventually acknowledge your integrity. Jesus of Nazareth was cursed at and mocked. He was spat upon, had His beard plucked out, was severely whipped, and had nails driven into His wrists and feet; He endured the worst form of capital punishment ever invented. Yet what did He say when He was dying on the cross? "Father, forgive them, for they do not know what they are doing."[4] Even after all He went through, Jesus perfectly reflected the Creator's nature—always consistent, predictable, trustworthy, just, and loving. That's character!

A true leader is able to take criticism and mistreatment and still retain his character.

Character Means…

Based on the above, let's look at some statements that summarize what it means to have character.

1. Character Means Having a Commitment to a Set of Values Without Compromise

Leaders of principle do not relinquish their values in the face of pressure to disregard their beliefs. Because their values are based on their convictions, they are willing to lose money, promotion, and other advantages for the sake of their values. Unfortunately, many leaders today are experts in compromise. They change their values based on what they think other people want them to do, not what they genuinely believe is right.

Moral compromise is different from the natural give-and-take that occurs, for instance, when a group of people is discussing options for how to implement procedures or what methods to use to attain a certain goal. There is an important distinction between compromising one's beliefs and making a concession on an opinion, so that a group can come to a consensus. In those circumstances, we are not to be uncompromising for its own sake, or for the purpose of making life hard for another individual. However, when moral issues are clearly at stake, we must steadfastly hold on to our values and ethical code.

In an earlier chapter, we discussed the account in which Moses sent twelve leaders to scope out the Promised Land before the nation of Israel entered it. Ten of the leaders expressed their fear of the inhabitants of the land, but two of them insisted the Israelites would be victorious over their enemies. These two leaders had a strong conviction about, and commitment to, what God had already assured them they could do. They had "a different spirit" from the other leaders.[5] They had the spirit of character.

Today, many leaders are afraid to be criticized and opposed, so they don't take a public stand on important moral issues that affect the well-being of their community and nation. They cannot handle disagreement, criticism, or opposition because they just want to be accepted. You could say they have accepted popularity as their "price" for moral compromise. When people try to pressure us to back off from our values, we have to be able to say, "I can't be 'bought,'" or "I'm not going to compromise," or "I must publicly express my principles regarding this issue." When you look back on your life, you may not remember the things that you fell for. But you will remember what you *stood* for.

2. Character Means Being Dedicated to a Set of Standards Without Wavering

Earlier, we examined the process through which our moral standards are derived from our values. We should compromise neither our values nor our standards. When a principled leader establishes moral parameters for his life, he doesn't waver in his dedication to them. He does not violate them for anyone or anything. As someone who has lived under the constant pressure of public scrutiny, let me tell you that no one else will set moral standards for you. You must set your own. And then you must be fixed and stable in relation to them.

Let me suggest a few additional examples of specific moral standards that a leader might set: "I will not lie in order to get a promotion or increase my profits"; "I will treat my employees justly by giving them fair wages and ensuring the safety of their work environment"; "I will uphold the value of every human life."

The first book of Moses gives the account of a young man named Joseph who lived in Canaan.[6] While he made some mistakes, he exhibited strong character dedicated to a set of moral standards that brought him through severe trials.

Joseph came from a large family. He was one of twelve sons—and his father's favorite. Consequently, his father gave him special treatment, including the gift of an elaborate robe. It's not surprising that his brothers became intensely jealous of him. After plotting to get rid of him for good, they sold him as a slave to a passing caravan that was on its way to Egypt. Then, they smeared the blood of a goat on his special robe to make their father think that Joseph had been attacked and killed by a wild animal.

How would you react if your own siblings sold you as a slave? Might not that have been an excuse to waver in regard to your standards? But Joseph relied on the reserves of his moral character, kept his wits about him, and trusted in God. He was purchased by a man named Potiphar, who was the captain of Pharaoh's guard. Even though he was a slave, Joseph apparently made a decision to perform his work with excellence, because Potiphar put him in charge of his entire household and everything he owned. Joseph established himself as a trusted and valued servant, and the estate prospered under his management.

So, life was improving for Joseph, and those are the times when some people will let their guard down and ride along where life is taking them, often becoming lax in their standards. If Joseph hadn't been unwavering in his convictions, that might have happened to him, too, because the opportunity soon presented itself. Joseph was good-looking, and he caught the eye of Potiphar's wife, who soon asked him to sleep with her! He refused, saying, "No one is greater in this house than I am. My master has withheld nothing from me except you, because you are his wife. How then could I do such a wicked thing and sin against God?"[7]

Even though she persisted *daily* in trying to convince him, he would not succumb to her offer. Again, how many people under such circumstances would have done the same? This young man was abruptly torn from his family and the home he'd always known and taken to a foreign land as a slave. He might have accepted whatever opportunities for pleasure and advantages were offered to him. Yet Joseph knew he had a noble purpose in life, and he had a reverence for his Creator, so he remained faithful to his ethical code.

His commitment cost him greatly. Furious at being refused, Potiphar's wife accused Joseph of attempting to molest her, and Potiphar had him thrown into prison. Remarkably, even in that circumstance, he must have remained steadfast, because the prison warden soon put him in charge of all the other prisoners. Every time he kept to his convictions, it strengthened his character even further.

So, Joseph remained dedicated to his principles, even though he was all but forgotten in prison. Yet all these trials were the prelude to his emergence as a powerful leader in Egypt when, through a series of God-orchestrated events, he went from imprisoned slave to Pharaoh's first-in-command. Keep Joseph's "character arc" in mind in the next chapter when we discuss how trials and difficulties lead to personal growth and steadfast integrity.

Every time Joseph kept to his convictions,
it strengthened his character even further.

---

3. Character Means Making a Continual Effort to Integrate Your Thoughts, Words, and Actions

Integrated Means "Whole" and "Entire"

The words *integrate* and *integrity* are both derived from the Latin word *integer*, meaning "whole" and "entire." Thus, one definition of *integrate* is "to form, coordinate, or blend into a functioning or unified whole." Having character means making a *continual* effort to integrate your thoughts, words, and actions, so that you are "one." A leader should be able to declare, "What I say, what I do, and who I am are the same." Achieving such consistency takes daily discipline.

An important principle to remember is that there's no "break" in life from character. There is no point at which we will have "arrived," so that we no longer have to concern ourselves with values and principles. We must therefore keep vigil over our character. For instance, it is very easy to be tempted to lie. Suppose you were laid off from your job, and you found some short-term work through a temporary agency. Then, at a social function, you meet a wealthy business executive who asks you, "So, what do you do for a living?" You don't want to seem inferior, so you inflate your job description. Character requires daily maintenance, because every day—and often many times throughout the day—our character will be tested.

Integrity Means Having One Face—Not Two or More

If we are to be principled leaders, our private life and our public life must be ethically "one." This means we must be honest when no one else is watching us. When we say something in public, we must still mean what we said when we are in private. A person with integrity is the same person all the time, night or day, hot or cold, in good times and in bad. He believes what he says, and he says what he believes. He says what he does, and he does what he says. There is no dichotomy.

When we lack integrity, we are disingenuous, or "two-faced." Let's look at an illustration of this concept from the origins of the acting profession. The Greeks were the first to develop drama. While they started out using only a chorus of people to narrate a story, they later incorporated into that format an individual who could play five different parts, or characters, by wearing different masks, changing them according to the particular role he was playing.

Interestingly, the word the Greeks used for this person was *hypokrites*, from which we get the English word *hypocrite*. Similarly, the word *hypocrisy* comes from the Greek word *hypokrisis*, meaning "acting on the stage, pretense," from *hypokrinesthai*, meaning "play a part, pretend."[8] In its original form, "hypocrite" was not a negative term; it merely referred to the actors who wore masks on the stage while playing multiple parts. However, the term evolved into the idea of a person of "many faces"—someone whose real identity was not what it appeared to be.

Jesus of Nazareth referred to a number of the religious leaders and practitioners of His day as "hypocrites." For example, He said, "So when you give to the needy, do not announce it with trumpets, as the hypocrites do in the synagogues and on the streets, to be honored by others. Truly I tell you, they have received their reward in full"[9]; and "Woe to you, teachers of the law and Pharisees, you hypocrites! You clean the outside of the cup and dish, but inside they are full of greed and self-indulgence."[10] In other words, He was saying, "You are actors! You wear a mask to hide who you really are. You keep changing your 'face.'" They were not "integrated" because they lacked true character.

We must ask ourselves, "Am I manifesting who I really am in my interactions with others?" That can be a tough question to ask yourself—and to answer—but it is a necessary one. We have to start taking off our masks, so that who we really are can be seen. Then, we must work to develop our character, so that other people will be able to fully trust what we say and do.

It is wearying to pretend to be someone you're not. It's as if you have more than one person living inside of you, working at cross-purposes. It's similar to what we talked about in an earlier chapter regarding character versus reputation. Character is who you are—reputation is the mask.

The problem with having a conversation with a hypocrite is that you're not sure exactly who you're speaking with at any given time. Today, many people—especially younger people—say, "Everybody is a hypocrite." They have observed too many leaders say one thing but do another. Or, they have seen leaders act in ways contrary to what they've been told constitutes good character. They don't believe that what the leaders tell them has any real value. As a result, many of them think, *I'll behave any way I want to, because standards don't seem to matter. Look at how that politician lied. Look at what that businessman stole.* They start pointing at people who have violated values and moral standards.

In contrast, when a leader's private life and his public life are consistent, he will demonstrate integrity to those around him. True character does not change with the tides; it is not altered according to the latest opinion poll. It is consistently "one."

The problem with having a conversation with a hypocrite is that you're not sure exactly who you're speaking with at any given time.

4. Character Means Making Sacrifices in Support of Your Principles

A principled leader possesses beliefs so strong that he is willing to sacrifice for them—to experience the loss of popularity, friendships, colleagues, financial gain, and success for their sake. Such a quality must be reintroduced to society by leaders of genuine principle.

Mahatma Gandhi made some major sacrifices for his vision. For instance, he went on several hunger strikes, one of which drew attention to the unjust treatment of India's poorest classes in the caste system, the "untouchables." People will continue to remember Gandhi for generations because of his willingness to sacrifice for what he believed in.

5. Character Means Imposing Self-Discipline in Keeping with Your Values and Moral Standards

In conjunction with making sacrifices, a leader must impose daily discipline upon himself, so that he will remain aligned with his convictions and continue to adhere to his principles. In chapter 5, we discussed specific ways to exercise self-discipline.

Perhaps, before you picked up this book, you felt like giving up your values and standards because you found yourself in the midst of a difficult circumstance. It could be that, because you had made a commitment to your principles, you disciplined yourself to stick with them, and affirmed, "I will continue to cultivate myself as a person and as a leader." If that has been your situation, I commend you for your discipline and urge you to keep holding on to your convictions. Your leadership is needed in our world!

The Manifestation of Character

As we have seen in this chapter, and as we will explore in more depth in chapter 10, character is manifested in our lives...

+ When our values, principles, morals, and standards are tested.

+ When we persevere under the pressures of life.

+ When self-sacrifice for the sake of our principles becomes more important to us than compromise for the sake of popularity.

Is your character fixed, set, predictable, and stable? Where will you be in five, ten, twenty, or thirty years? Will you continue to follow moral standards, or will you have sacrificed them on the altar of compromise? Will you still hold to the same convictions, or will you have abandoned them for temporary pleasure?

Some years ago, I visited another country to speak at a conference held at the church of a famous preacher in that nation. The church was packed with people, and it was a good experience. The preacher introduced me to his spouse, whom he called "my darling, beautiful wife, to whom I've been married all these years." The next year, when I went back, he had a different wife. He had divorced his first wife to marry someone else.

I never went back to that church, because I couldn't trust the man. If he couldn't keep his word to his own spouse, how do I know he would keep his word to me? (He is now on his third wife.) Instead of having true character, this man *was* a character. He was wearing a mask. There are many people like that in the world. We don't want to *be* a character; we want to *have* character.

Each of us must take some responsibility for the crisis of character in our world today. We are all part of the problem. But we can all be part of the solution by committing to follow sound principles and moral standards—to becoming "one" in our thoughts, words, and actions. To quote Winston Churchill's famous declaration: "Never give in, never give in, *never, never, never, never*—in nothing, great or small, large or petty—never give in except to convictions of honour and good sense."[11]

10

Tempting Your Character

"Laws and principles are not for the times when there is no temptation: they are for such moments as this, when body and soul rise in mutiny against their rigour....If at my convenience I might break them, what would be their worth?"
—Charlotte Brontë, *Jane Eyre*

On a trip to Israel, I toured a site where ancient artifacts from the Roman Empire were on display. In one area of the site, I noticed what looked like a large smelting pot, as well as pieces of metal, a broken sword, a broken dagger, and an intact sword. The guide at the site explained, "The Roman Empire had the most powerful army in the world. Practically no one defeated the Romans militarily. Why? They not only had superior strategy, but they also had superior weapons. And the reason Roman swords were so powerful is that they had been properly tempered."

The guide then explained the tempering process. A Roman blacksmith would take iron ore and beat it on an anvil with a steel mallet to make it flat and even. Then, he would put the metal in a furnace. When the metal became red-hot from the fire, the blacksmith would be able to detect dark spots in it, which indicated areas of weakness. Wherever he saw a spot, he would hammer at it until he couldn't see it anymore. Then, he'd take the glowing metal and thrust it in very cold water. This caused all the molecules in the metal to move close together, strengthening it.

After this, the blacksmith would take the sword out of the water and put it back in the fire. The metal would heat up again, and he would check the area where he had previously worked on the spot. If it was still there, he kept working at it until it was completely gone. Then, he'd put the sword back in the fire until it was glowing hot again, so he could identify the other weak areas. He would repeat this process until no more spots remained. In this way, the sword would repeatedly be subjected to a process that took it from burning fire to hammering to ice-cold water.

The guide said that whenever a blacksmith finished making a sword, he engraved his own name or mark on it. So, every Roman sword identified the person who had forged it. And every blacksmith who worked for the Roman army had a contract stipulating that if any of his swords broke, he could be put to death.

This guarantee that the sword would not break was crucial to the success and safety of the soldiers. They were going out into the world of battle. And when they were in the middle of the pressures of combat, they couldn't afford to have their swords break. If they did, their lives could be jeopardized. The soldiers had to be able to place confidence in the strength and durability of their weapons. And the only way they could trust their swords was to know that they had gone through this "tempering" process.

Strengthened Through Trials

The verb *temper* may be defined as "to make stronger and more resilient through hardship." The process of tempering swords may be compared to a process that is essential to the building of our character—this is the process of being *tempted*.

You may be thinking, *What? Isn't being tempted something to avoid?*

We must realize that being tempted is not the same as *succumbing* to temptation. The process of temptation reveals what is genuine in our character and what is false, similar to the process of refining gold in fire, in which everything that isn't pure gold is burned away. Believe me, friend: Every day of your life, your character will be tested! These tests are not for the purpose of defeating us but rather for strengthening us.

You probably already know many of your strengths, but are you aware of all your weaknesses? Each of us has weak areas in our character. And testing, or tempering, has much more to do with checking for our weaknesses than for our strengths. The Roman blacksmiths would start out with weak, porous pieces of metal when crafting their swords. That condition of the metal describes the inner state of human beings, who contend with the effects of fallen humanity. To be tempted is to be assessed for moral weaknesses—"spots"—in our character, so they can be removed, and so we can become leaders of principle. And as our character is strengthened, we will prove our trustworthiness to lead others.

> *To be tempted is to be assessed for moral weaknesses—*
> *"spots"—in our character, so they can be removed,*
> *and so we can become leaders of principle.*

Paul of Tarsus wrote the following to his first-century audience in Rome about the process of character building: "We also rejoice in our sufferings, because we know that suffering produces perseverance; perseverance, character; and character, hope. And hope does not disappoint us...."[1] Isn't that powerful? The Greek word for *character* in this passage indicates "the process or result of trial, proving, approval."[2] What a process! I consider it the secret to character development.

The word "sufferings" here can be equated to tests and challenges. Paul was saying that when we go through trials, we will build perseverance. To persevere means to bear up under pressure, so that we remain consistent and stable. We should view each temptation as an opportunity to strengthen the weak areas of our lives.

Resisting temptation and enduring in the midst of trials can seem like daunting tasks. However, as one biblical writer emphasized, "No discipline seems pleasant at the time, but painful. Later on, however, it produces a harvest of righteousness and peace for those who have been trained by it."[3] We never know how strong or stable we are until we're under real pressure. When life heats up in the course of various difficulties and trials, our weaknesses become exposed, allowing us to see them clearly. Instead of turning away from what we see, we must acknowledge those flaws. Then, to get back on the right track, we need to determine the appropriate ethical principle to apply and then align ourselves with it through personal discipline. We must allow the tempering process to train us. As we do, we will recommit ourselves to our convictions, values, and moral standards, strengthening our character.

Intentional Personal Development

Character is manifested when our values, principles, morals, and standards are tested. And life will give us plenty of tests. However, the challenges and trials that come to us from external forces will not address all of our weaknesses. Therefore, just as the blacksmith sought out the weak areas of the metal, character building involves self-evaluation. We should be intentional about assessing ourselves according to the established moral principles to which we have committed. Wherever we find a "spot," we should work to eliminate it. When we have addressed a character flaw for a period of time, we should search for another. This can be hard work, but it is worth it!

As we have seen, our character cannot be developed unless we make a personal commitment to our convictions and moral standards. We also need to specifically state these convictions and standards—first to ourselves, and then to our families, our colleagues, our constituents, our communities, and so forth. This is when we make declarations such as, "I will/will not do such and such." When you state your values, standards, and code of ethics to yourself, you reinforce your convictions and encourage personal discipline in relation to them. However, you must be aware that when you make a commitment to a moral standard and declare that you will uphold it, you give "life" the right to remind you of it in the tests and challenges it hands you. It's as if life says, "You told me that you believe this—now prove it. I'm going to test you."

When you state your values, standards,
and code of ethics to yourself, you reinforce your convictions
and encourage personal discipline.

Peter, one of Jesus of Nazareth's disciples—His leaders-in-training—said to Him, "I am ready to go with you to prison and to death."[4] In other words, "I will never compromise my values; I will never violate Your trust. In fact, I am willing to sacrifice my life for You." Jesus knew His disciple's weaknesses. He explained to Peter that not only was he not yet committed to sacrifice for his beliefs by going to prison and to death, but he would even deny Him three times. That is why He previously told Peter, in effect, "The adversary (Satan) will try to sift you like wheat, but I have prayed for you, so that you will retain your faith." (In other words, I have prayed that your convictions will not collapse in the midst of your tests.) "Then, when you come through this, and your own character is strengthened, use this experience to help others strengthen their character."[5] When we fail life's tests, we must learn from them. We must not give up our core beliefs and convictions but recommit to act in accordance with them.

There can be no "secret" or private moral codes in a leader's life. There may be times when individuals need to strengthen their personal character for a season before announcing their convictions to the world, so that they won't fail publicly if they have a number of character issues to work on. But, at some point, a leader's convictions must become public knowledge. All great leaders face opposition to their convictions. They don't experience this opposition by keeping their ethical values a secret. It happens because they commit to their values and express them openly, and because their words are reinforced by their actions.

Our character, then, is forged in the public declaration of our values and moral standards. Suppose Mahatma Gandhi had never spoken publicly of his convictions about the dignity and equality of all human beings. He might have earned a good living and had a fairly happy—and safe—life as a lawyer. However, he never would have achieved greatness by helping the people of his country to achieve self-rule.

As you've progressed through this book, have you become aware of your own ethical weaknesses? If so, that's a good thing. Again, only when we see our ethical "spots" can we remove them. For example, you may be saying, "I have been compromising in my personal life. No more! I'm not going to date that person anymore. He is not encouraging me to hold to moral standards." You shouldn't be surprised if your new commitment is tested immediately. So, prepare yourself.

Years ago, a young woman came to me and said, "Dr. Munroe, I heard one of your teachings, and you were talking about how to set disciplines and standards for your life. I decided I was going to live that way, because I want to be an upright person." Then she said that, the day after she made that commitment, an old boyfriend she hadn't seen for twenty years just happened to get on the elevator she was riding. She told me, "And he was looking good! I'm forty-two years old and still single, and he made me a tempting offer." This offer was not in keeping with moral standards, so I asked, "What did you do?" And she said, "I ran to you—help me!" I told her that, ultimately, no one else can assist us to keep our character. They can encourage us and challenge us, but we have to take responsibility for our actions and apply personal discipline.

Allowing life to expose our ethical flaws, and intentionally rooting out our weaknesses, are ongoing processes that make us more and more ethically resilient. This means that we're always in one stage or another of development—we're either hot, cold, or getting hammered at! When will our individual spots be fully pounded out? When we have proven to be trustworthy in the corresponding areas.

We're always in one stage or another of development—
we're either hot, cold, or getting hammered at!

The Distinguishing Mark of Character

The following are several key concepts related to character development, or the "tempering" process:

+ The distinguishing mark of a leader is character.

+ The distinguishing mark of character is trustworthiness.

+ Trustworthiness is a product of stability established through tests over time.

A leader becomes trustworthy by staying consistent in character as he undergoes tests and trials over the course of time. Your trustworthiness is established when you have been tested over a long period—with such difficulties as changing circumstances, vocational challenges, personal crises, and temptations—and have either passed the tests or learned from them so you can pass them in the future.

Remember that a principled leader is fixed, predictable, and stable. Because a leader's character is developed as he stays steady and strong through tests and trials, people trust him on the basis of the tests he has come through, not merely by what he says. If you lose the trust of your followers, you've lost your followers—period. That is why the ultimate pursuit of a leader should be character, not skill, power, influence, or anything else.

Whether we are fully aware of it or not, life tests us to see if we have developed such qualities as responsibleness, competence, loyalty, honesty, fairness, and goodwill. We don't know what our true character is until it has been tested. We don't know who we really are until we have been tempted to compromise.

Here are some of the areas in which our character will be tested:

1. Our commitment, or standards, in relation to something or someone.

2. Our loyalty to our convictions when we are under pressure.

3. Our dedication to the values we promised we would never violate.

4. Our faithfulness to what is right and just.

5. Our honesty and integrity.

Our character cannot mature unless we are tested and tempted. We must accept the fact that the tempering process is necessary if we want to cultivate moral force. When we go through trials, we often wonder, "Why is this happening to me?" It's part of our leadership training in character.

Establishing Trustworthiness

Jesus of Nazareth experienced many tests and trials, and one of the most demanding was at the beginning of His public ministry, when He was thirty years old. Let us look at an account of what transpired, written by one of Jesus' disciples. It begins, "Then Jesus was led by the Spirit into the desert to be tempted...."[6] The word "Spirit" in this passage has a capital "S." That means that God Himself led Jesus into the desert to be tempted, or "tempered." He tested His own Son for the purpose of trying His character. Let us continue the account:

> After fasting forty days and forty nights [in the desert], [Jesus] was hungry. The tempter came to him and said, "If you are the Son of God, tell these stones to become bread." Jesus answered, "It is written: 'Man does not live on bread alone, but on every word that comes from the mouth of God.'" Then the devil took him to the holy city and had him stand on the highest point of the temple. "If you are the Son of God," he said, "throw yourself down. For it is written: 'He will command his angels concerning you, and they will lift you up in their hands, so that you will not strike your foot against a stone.'" Jesus answered him, "It is also written: 'Do not put the Lord your God to the test.'" Again, the devil took him to a very high mountain and showed him all the kingdoms of the world and their splendor. "All this I will give you," he said, "if you will bow down and worship me." Jesus said to him, "Away from me, Satan! For it is written: 'Worship the Lord your God, and serve him only.'"[7]

God's enemy, Satan, is the enemy of humanity, as well. In the Bible, he is referred to variously as "the tempter," "the devil," and "the accuser," and he, too, tests us for weakness. He did this with the first human beings when he told them the Creator was acting in an unjust way toward them and tempted them to violate a vital principle. As we discussed, the first man and woman failed this test.

God allows the tempter to test us as part of the tempering process, which is meant to show us our vulnerable areas so that we might seek to be strengthened and established in character. As the first-century writer James expressed, "When tempted, no one should say, 'God is tempting me.' For God cannot be tempted by evil, nor does he tempt anyone; but each one is tempted when, by his own evil desire, he is dragged away and enticed."[8]

As the tempering process builds our character, we become more and more trustworthy. For instance, being criticized by other people is a test we all experience. Yet our critics can be among our greatest assets, because criticism always puts our character on trial for its authenticity and shows us the true state of our thoughts and attitudes.

Satan will not tempt us in the areas of our lives in which he knows we are strong. Rather, he tests us in the areas in which we are unstable or about which we are uncertain. And, every time we resist temptation in an area of weakness, we fortify that area with character. Suppose you are trying to break a bad habit. If, every time the habit attempts to assert itself, you "hammer" it, your character in that area will be strengthened. Eventually, you will overcome the habit and no longer be tempted in that area. But stay alert—the tempting will begin in a different area!

Our critics can be among our greatest assets, because criticism always puts our character on trial for its authenticity and shows us the true state of our thoughts and attitudes.

Here's another example of a type of test that may come your way. Suppose you are returning to your home country after having traveled overseas. The customs officer asks you, "Do you have any goods to declare?" For five seconds, you feel the intense pressure of a test, because you are tempted to tell a lie so that you that won't have to pay any customs duties. You think you might get away with it. Then you remember that one of the moral standards you have committed to is, "I will be honest in all my business dealings." So, you say, "Yes, sir, I have several items to declare."

Once, when I arrived home from a trip out of the country, I made my way to the customs desk at the airport. I am well-known in my nation, and the customs officer said, "That's okay; you don't need to declare that." I replied, "No, it's not okay. I don't want you to give me any special treatment. Let me pay." •

A leader's position and title do not exempt him from being honest. We don't have the right to violate principles just because an opportunity to cut corners or make money illegally presents itself. Suppose you obtained a position as the head of a government department that awarded contracts in the areas of engineering and construction. You have three hundred million dollars in your budget. Suddenly, you experience intense pressure, because many of your friends and casual acquaintances begin to call you, asking to be granted contracts. But the hardest test comes when your uncle approaches you with a tear in his eye, telling you that things are financially tough, and he can't pay his rent. He wants you to grant him a lucrative contract. You know he's not qualified to be given a contract, and it would be a conflict of interest, but you are tempted to compromise your principles and misspend public funds for the sake of helping your father's brother.

•Let me emphasize that there is no one in the world for whom you should give up your integrity. In many instances, if you compromise your convictions to please someone else, you'll be amazed at how little that person cares. He will use you, and then dismiss you. Or, he will leave you to pick up the pieces. Then, you will have to live with the fact that you compromised your moral standards. Again, leaders fail when they sacrifice their character on the altar of compromise.

Jesus passed each one of the tempter's tests without compromising His integrity. That doesn't mean it wasn't painful for Him to experience those tests. But His commitment was steadfast—He remained true to His values and principles, citing them in response to each argument of temptation made by Satan.

Note that in the process of trying to get Jesus to violate His principles, Satan endeavored to make Jesus doubt His position. The tempter also distorted the meaning of one of the principles God had established. The principle he twisted would have been valid in context, but he used it out of context. Yet, because Jesus had a thorough knowledge of the Creator's principles, He was able to see through the tempter's deception and effectively refute him.

We must be aware that the same experience could happen to us. Other people—or the tempter himself—may try to make us doubt our position in God or twist the meaning of first laws in order to get us to compromise our beliefs and values. For example, someone may say, "The Bible says, 'Beloved, I pray that you may prosper in all things and be in health, just as your soul prospers.'[9] You're supposed to prosper in all things, so what's wrong with taking a little money under the table? Everyone does it!" To which you should reply, "The Bible also says, 'You shall not steal.'"[10]

The temptations that Jesus of Nazareth experienced in the desert reflect the three major types of temptations that all human beings experience in life: (1) The test of the appetites—such as for excess food and drink; illegal drugs and other addictive substances; and lust, or uncontrolled passion—whether physical or emotional; (2) the test of fame; and (3) the test of power. Every leader who has fallen has been snared by at least one of these three.

The three major types of temptations that all human beings experience are the test of the appetites, the test of fame, and the test of power.

The second temptation the tempter tried on Jesus was essentially this: "Jump off the building and land like Superman! People will be dazzled, and You'll be an instant success." Leaders who rise quickly in fame, power, and/ or fortune are often referred to as "overnight successes."

I do believe in overnight success—if the "night" lasts about twenty-five years! Principled leaders usually go through a long process of character building and persevering in their leadership vision, during which they faithfully keep their commitments, pursue their goals, refine their skills, and develop their trustworthiness. This process leads to personal success that is grounded and lasting. However, many who become successful overnight end up instant failures not long afterward. Think of what happens to the majority of people who win the lottery. They squander their winnings quickly, and many are worse off than they were before they had wealth.

So, don't jump from the pinnacle of the building. Instead, take the long walk that leads you through places of testing, where your character can be tried and proven. Then, you can come out on the other side as a successful leader, both personally and professionally, experiencing longevity and leaving a lasting legacy.

The Trust Exchange

We should never take our leadership role lightly, because people are observing us as we go through various tests and trials in the tempering process. They are watching our lives, our marriages, our attitudes, and our manner of conducting ourselves when we work. And if we become ethically shaky, or shadowy, in these areas, we will lose the most important gift a leader has—the trust of his followers.

The Currency of True Leadership Is Trust

In any economy, transactions between producers and consumers cannot occur without the exchange of some form of legitimate currency—money, goods, the promise of a percentage of profits, and so forth. Likewise, leaders must have the indispensable currency of trust in order to enter into corporate agreement with their followers and/or the members of their group. Trust is like an account that people make deposits into on our behalf, based on our character. Without the currency of trust, we cannot function as leaders. In fact, without trust, we have no leadership.

Trust Is the Product of Character

You *cannot* lead people who don't trust you. As a leader, you must accept that fact right now, if you haven't already done so. If people don't trust you, they will ignore you, resist you, even sabotage your leadership. The account of trust that a leader has established between himself and his followers should be considered sacred. Accordingly, your personal decisions should be such that they protect the confidence your followers have placed in you. Otherwise, you could lose all the currency of trust you have accumulated to this point.

Your trust as a leader is earned and maintained by the consistency you exhibit as you go through various tests over time, such as we have been discussing in this chapter—tests of faithfulness, reliability, consistency, and so forth. People will observe how you go through various challenges and trials, in order to determine what your true character is. When they see that you stay steady, they will make a deposit of trust into your leadership account. When they see that you remain faithful, they will make another deposit. When you prove your reliability, they will place additional currency into your account. However, if you were to violate the people's faith in you, you couldn't buy their trust. Your account would probably have to be closed, because the deposits would stop immediately. You could no longer transact leadership business with your (former) followers.

Your trust as a leader is earned and maintained by the consistency you exhibit as you go through various tests over time.

Character is moral force that convinces people you are someone who has earned the right to be heard and followed. In this way, great leadership is not attained by pursuing greatness but by persevering through great tests. Your character will be defined by the tests you have endured.

Let Your True Character Emerge

Right now—or sometime soon—you may feel as if you've had the heat turned up beneath you, followed by the impression that you are being hammered by trials, followed by the sensation of being plunged into an icy sea of trouble. If so, you may be experiencing one of the most significant periods of your life. Though you are being challenged, you can appreciate where the challenge will take you, now that you understand the tempering process. Tell yourself, "I'm going to make it through the fire, the pounding, and the freezing water!" Character is developed through pressure, demands, temptations, and resolve. It is my hope that, as your character undergoes various tests and trials, you will become a principled leader who makes a remarkable difference in your organization.

At times, life throws us some heavy disappointments. But we shouldn't allow them to defeat us. In chapter 9, we looked at various illustrations of what it means to have fixed, predictable, stable character. One of those was the example of a statue, which provides us with another important image that corresponds to the tempering process.

As I said previously, the statue of Queen Victoria in Parliament Square in Nassau is carved out of solid marble. Yet what we must keep in mind is that the statue didn't always look the way it does now. Before the sculptor created the image, it was "hidden" in a big block of rock. But I picture this artist walking around that block and saying, "There's someone in there—I can see her clearly!" That's because the artist could envision a beautiful piece of sculpture underneath the plain surface of the marble.

The same concept holds true for us. At times, we may not look like much to ourselves. We may become discouraged about the exercise of our leadership and the process of our character development, so that our vision of our future becomes blocked. But our Creator is saying, "There's someone in there—I can see him clearly!" He sees our potential; He sees the promise He's placed within us. He sees the finished product—a leader of character.

The only way the sculptor could prove the potential of that block of marble was to pick up a piece of steel and a heavy chisel and begin applying pressure, skillfully chipping away at the stone over the course of weeks and months. He had to keep working with that piece of marble so that "Queen Victoria" could emerge. If the developing statue could feel and speak, she'd say it was a painful process. As the fragments were chiseled away, she would have called out, "Stop! That hurts!" When big chunks fell off, she would have thought, *I'm not going to survive this!*

Similarly, there are times when we experience sustained periods of difficulty, when everything seems to be falling apart in our lives. We feel pressure that is so intense, it's as if we're being shown no mercy. We think, *This isn't fair!* At such times, we must let our beliefs, convictions, and values tell us, "Stay steady; hold on."

Then—bam!—life will hit us again, and we'll say, "I don't think I'm going to survive!" But that's the point when we must allow our moral discipline to reply, "You're going to be okay. You are still standing." Sometimes, when big "pieces" drop from our own lives—jobs, close relationships, comfortable positions—we feel like we're losing part of ourselves. However, we must let our character say, "That aspect of your life was holding you back, and you needed to be free of it to emerge a true leader."

"Queen Victoria" endured much chiseling and the loss of what surrounded her—but for the purpose of becoming a beautiful sculpture. We, too, are "artistic projects" of our Creator. For too long, we've been hiding underneath our character flaws. Yet the process of character development will reveal who we really are—who we were always meant to be. We were created to be strong, steady, and noble leaders, fulfilling our purpose and vision with excellence.

Sometimes, people have not yet reached their leadership goals because their character needs to be developed more first. They will arrive at their destination if they persevere. Some people want to be in the public eye too soon, when there are still negative "chunks" of their lives that need to fall away. I've gone through more than four decades of being "chiseled" and having the excess "rock" broken off of my life. This ongoing process has given me stability; it has caused me to become established in my life and leadership.

So, be grateful for the chiseling and the hammering—the trials and tribulations of life. Give thanks for the process of tempering. Allow every stress, problem, and challenging circumstance to further prepare you to fulfill your leadership vision.

11

Core Qualities
of Principled Leaders

*"Good character is not formed in a week or a month. It is created
little by little, day by day. Protracted and patient effort is needed
to develop good character."*
—Heraclitus, Greek philosopher

To be effective leaders, we must cultivate many important attitudes
and characteristics, such as courage, passion, initiative, patience,
teamwork, wisdom, and persistence. But there are several core qualities
that we must focus on as we make character our priority in leadership. In
this chapter, we will take a brief overview of these qualities, so that we can
be intentional about building them into our lives.

Strong Convictions

In chapter 3 and elsewhere in this book, we discussed the necessity of
forming strong convictions. However, this process is so central to the development of character that it merits being included in this chapter, as well.
As we have seen, convictions refer to two aspects of leadership: (1) a leader's
certainty that he has a unique purpose in life, and (2) his wholehearted
personal commitment to a vision worth sacrificing for.

Our established belief system gives rise to our convictions. To have
convictions is to sense that there is something we *must* do while we are on
this earth. It is not optional, because life will have no meaning if we don't

accomplish it. As I wrote earlier, we can learn all the skills, methods, and styles of leadership, but they won't mean much if we have no real convictions that guide our lives, or if we sell out those convictions.

Accountability

Accountability, or answering to a higher authority for our attitudes and actions, reflects a commitment to our own personal integrity. This core quality helps us to remain fixed, set, predictable, and stable in character. We have a responsibility to be accountable on three levels—to ourselves, to other people, and to our Creator.

A Commitment to Self-evaluation

First, we are responsible for regularly examining our own conduct to assess if we are living according to the moral principles that we value highly and have established as standards for ourselves. Again, we can accomplish this most effectively if we have written down our principles, beliefs, convictions, values, moral standards, and ethical code, so that we can easily refer to them.

A Commitment to Evaluation by Others

Second, to be accountable means to submit the evaluation of our attitudes and actions to another individual or group of individuals qualified to examine them in light of the principles to which we have committed. No one can see all of his own weaknesses, or the areas of his life in which he may be compromising his standards. We all sometimes need a different perspective on our lives to show us our weaknesses and our strengths alike. That is why many people have "accountability partners" with whom they meet regularly to encourage and challenge each other.

We should make ourselves accountable only to someone of proven character who has demonstrated that he has our best interests at heart. He should be someone who is able to clearly assess our progress in character development and show us how to get back on track when we have strayed. When we are able to take an honest look at our character, and commit to work on our areas of weakness, we will strengthen our integrity. We will integrate our thoughts, words, and actions even further, so they can become "one." ◂

A principled leader truly welcomes this process of accountability. He desires to have his values tested for consistency. He wants to know how well he is holding to his own stated code of ethics. Rather than being afraid of constructive criticism, he embraces appraisal because he understands that his inherent worth was given to him by his Creator. Because he desires to manifest true character, he is strong enough to hear what he needs to hear and to use it profitably in his life.

In contrast, unprincipled leaders are afraid of being held accountable, so they avoid evaluation whenever possible. As a result, many of them become "lone wolves." They think, *I'm accountable only to myself.* Such people risk self-deception and isolation from the community of which they are a part. They may also begin to use and misuse other people.

In many organizations, leaders are accountable to a board of directors, a group of advisors, or a similar accountability group. If they do not have such a forum to hold them responsible for their stated values, principles, and goals, leaders can make bad moral choices and other unwise decisions. Many leaders fall due to a lack of accountability, as we have seen in the examples throughout this book. A number of them had apparently not made an intentional decision to pursue character-based leadership, so they had never really submitted themselves to either self-examination or evaluation by a board or other group.

Finally, a commitment to evaluation by others means that a leader reports not only to those *to whom* he is responsible but also to those *for whom* he is responsible. Accordingly, he should regularly meet with his followers to make sure he is supporting them as they work to fulfill their part of the vision. And he should endeavor to supply whatever they may need in this regard.

A Commitment to Evaluation by the Creator

Third, a principled leader recognizes that his ultimate accountability is to God. That is why he has made a commitment to follow the Creator's first laws. He knows that even when he is alone, everything he says and does is observed by his Higher Authority.

As beings created in the image and likeness of God, we have responsibilities and privileges alike. One of our responsibilities is to "fear" our Creator. The term "the fear of the Lord," which is found in the Bible, does not mean that we are to be afraid of Him. In this sense, the word "fear" has to do with a great reverence and respect for Him that causes us to desire to follow His principles. It also refers to a proper sense of respect for His power, His love, and His other qualities.

We each have gifts and talents, but we did not create ourselves, and this fact should cause us to put our accomplishments into perspective and to express gratitude to our Creator for them. In chapter 9, we looked at the story of a young man named Joseph who had been sold into slavery by his brothers and later falsely accused and imprisoned. Joseph is an example of a leader with great reverence for God. The reason he was moved from the prison to the palace was that God had given him the ability to understand the meaning of significant dreams. When Pharaoh had a troubling dream, someone remembered Joseph's gift, and he was sent for by the Egyptian ruler.

Let's examine what Pharaoh said to Joseph, and then what Joseph's response was. "Pharaoh said to Joseph, 'I had a dream, and no one can interpret it. But I have heard it said of you that when you hear a dream you can interpret it.'"[1] Wouldn't you feel good if a king said that to you, especially if you'd just spent years in prison for being unjustly convicted of a crime? You would want to enjoy the moment and take credit for your ability. Yet, because Joseph revered God, he understood his responsibility to acknowledge the source of his gift. "'I cannot do it,' Joseph replied to Pharaoh, 'but God will give Pharaoh the answer he desires.'"[2] A principled leader doesn't stand up in such a situation and say, "I'm the answer to all your problems!" Rather, he gives credit where it is due.

A leader's willingness to be accountable reflects his commitment to always be consistent in what he says, what he does, and who he is. Accountability—in all three realms we've just discussed—protects a leader from being hypocritical, or two-faced, enabling him to align his life with his standards and principles and to establish his character.

A leader's willingness to be accountable reflects his commitment to be consistent in what he says, what he does, and who he is.

Monitoring Your Associations

Let me mention one other subject related to accountability. When we do not exercise discernment about those whom we choose to be our close friends and associates, we can inadvertently become answerable to people who don't have our best interests in mind, and whose immature character may have a negative effect on us. Consequently, we may end up following unwise advice and false principles. As I mentioned earlier, our character— for good or ill—often determines the nature of the people who gravitate to us and become our companions. In other words, our character determines our company. We should form friendships with those who value what we value and are committed to principled living. For this reason, we must be intentional about choosing our close associates, as well as developing our personal character.

Humility

The next core quality is humility. The word *humble* is derived from the Latin word *humus*, meaning "earth." To be humble, then, means to be "down-to-earth." In the context of character, this means to express and manifest your true self in accordance with your unique, inherent purpose. A leader can manifest true humility only after he accepts his significance as a person and as a leader. When he does so, he ceases to be self-conscious about his actions. He evaluates them regularly, but he does not strive at them, and he does not pretend to be someone he is not. If an individual "tries" to be humble, he has missed the true meaning of humility. If we're not manifesting our true selves, we cannot be humble. We have inadvertently put on a mask that hides what we are meant to express and reveal to the world.

The quality of humility in a leader is manifested through "servant leadership." Previously, we discussed Jesus of Nazareth's description of the difference between the Roman leaders and the leaders in the "kingdom of God." The Romans leaders liked to lord it over people, ordering them around. But Jesus said that whoever wants to become great must serve other people. Ordering people around is not the spirit of a true leader. Are your family members, employees, or colleagues afraid of you? If so, that fact shouldn't make you feel better about yourself. Likewise, you shouldn't get joy out of an ability to order people around. That is the wrong spirit. A principled leader has an attitude, or spirit, of service.

When a leader is humble, he also has a healthy attitude toward the areas of his life in which he still needs to grow in character. I've previously quoted from the writings and sayings of Abraham Lincoln. Lincoln is an example of a strong but humble leader. He was intelligent, wise, and perceptive. But he was also unpretentious, even as president, and he would often express that quality through his self-deprecating humor. On one occasion, a man attempted to curry favor with Lincoln by informing him that his secretary of war, Edwin Stanton, had called him a fool. Lincoln responded that Stanton was usually right, and that he would give the comment some thought! Lincoln was comfortable with himself, and he did not feel the need to defend himself whenever criticism came his way.

Leaders who don't understand their inherent purpose and worth have difficulty being humble because they often need reassurance through the praise of others. But leaders of principle have found something greater than other people's accolades—they have found a personal "assignment," or vision, and they are busy pursuing it. They are occupied with being who they were created to be, so they don't feel a need to be continually puffed up by others.

Similarly, when we are genuinely humble, we are less likely to be controlled by other people's opinions of us. We can't be leaders of character if we are always afraid of what other people will think or say of us. Some people mistake timidity for the quality of humility, but they are opposites: Timidity is related to fear, while humility is related to peace—peace with oneself and peace with other people.

When we are genuinely humble, we are less likely to be controlled by other people's opinions of us.

One way to gauge your fear of other people is to evaluate the way you talk to your boss or someone else in authority when you have a problem or concern. If you have an issue you want to discuss, do you tell your boss exactly what's wrong, how you feel about it, and what you recommend be done to solve it? I'm not suggesting that you be argumentative but that you have a reasoned, well-thought-out presentation. When we are afraid of authority figures, we are often not honest with them, and we often do not obtain the help and results we need. A fear of other people will undermine our character and hinder the fulfillment of our vision and goals.

Perhaps the following scenario will seem familiar to you. When preparing to discuss an issue with their boss, some people rehearse what they're going to say ahead of time, on their commute to work. They might go over their statement again in front of the mirror in the restroom. But then, when they get into their boss's office, their fear of authority makes them either freeze up or stumble over their words, so that they never say what they intended to say. Instead, they might just tell him they came in to say hello and wish him a good day. But somebody who has confidence in his own inherent worth and abilities will not fear authority. He will approach him in a practical and confident way.

There is a proverb that begins, "Fear of man will prove to be a snare...."[3] A snare, or trap, is something in which you are caught and from which it is difficult to escape. We do not have to fear people just because they have a certain title or hold a particular office. If you are afraid of authority, and you haven't been promoted at your job as quickly as you thought you should be, perhaps the managers at your workplace see you as someone who lacks confidence and would not be able to handle additional responsibilities. Whatever the reason, you can overcome your fear of man by focusing on fulfilling your inherent purpose and seeking to serve others.

Integrity

One definition of integrity is "incorruptibility." If you are incorruptible, you will not be enticed by your own desires or the pressure of other people to violate your moral standards or to operate on the basis of self-interest. Integrity was a quality exemplified by George Washington; he demonstrated that he could not be corrupted by power.

At the time that the American Revolution ended, King George III of England was having his portrait painted by artist Benjamin West. He asked the painter what he thought George Washington would do now that the war was concluded. West replied that he thought Washington would resign and go back to his farm. A startled King George exclaimed, "If he does that, he will be the greatest man in the world!"

To give up power voluntarily at the height of success and popular support is a rare decision for a leader, making his action even more impressive. Likewise, after Washington had served two terms as president of the United States, he did not run for a third term, because he had accepted the office in order to serve the people, not to garner power for himself. Washington was so highly regarded for his integrity that a number of Americans of his time would have supported the idea of giving him a life term as president, or even making him king. Instead, he calmly passed the reins of office to the next elected president. In doing so, he set a standard for all presidents to come, and helped to stabilize the new nation.

It is said that Napoleon Bonaparte, the famous military leader and former emperor of France, made a telling comment as he sat out his second exile on the island of Elba, lamenting his fall from power. He said that the people of France had "wanted him to be another George Washington." But he could not do it. Because he loved power, he never would have given it up of his own accord.

Responsibleness

Leaders of principle also act responsibly, and they eagerly accept responsibility. One of the Creator's first laws is that if we are faithful over the smaller jobs and tasks we have been given, we will be granted even greater ones.[4] This is the process by which leaders grow into increasingly responsible positions.

The process usually starts with the leader's own initiative to assume responsibility. Some people are annoyed by the thought of having to work.

They don't want people to ask them to do anything—whether it's helping out with chores at home, doing the "grunt" work at a volunteer organization, taking care of the paperwork related to their job, or something else. Frankly, many people are lazy. But a principled leader loves responsibility. ◆ He welcomes the opportunity to be productive and often looks for useful • work to do.

In this regard, let's look at one more example from the life of Joseph. Joseph successfully interpreted Pharaoh's dream, which was a message to the ruler and his nation that seven years of plenty would come, but they would be followed by seven years of famine. When Pharaoh heard the interpretation, he immediately said to Joseph:

> Since God has made all this known to you, there is no one so discerning and wise as you. You shall be in charge of my palace, and all my people are to submit to your orders. Only with respect to the throne will I be greater than you....I hereby put you in charge of the whole land of Egypt.[5]

If there ever was a time when Joseph might have felt he could delegate his work and finally take it a little easy, this would have been it! Instead, he • worked diligently in his new role, preparing for the days of famine:

> And Joseph went out from Pharaoh's presence and traveled throughout Egypt. During the seven years of abundance the land produced plentifully. Joseph collected all the food produced in those seven years of abundance in Egypt and stored it in the cities. In each city he put the food grown in the fields surrounding it. Joseph stored up huge quantities of grain, like the sand of the sea; it was so much that he stopped keeping records because it was beyond measure.[6]

In contrast to Joseph's responsible attitude, some people seek to avoid their boss, the head of their volunteer organization, their pastor, their parents, and so forth, because they don't want to be put into a situation where they will be asked to *do* something. However, though many of these people will avoid working at smaller tasks, they suddenly appear when an important and exciting opportunity comes along. Then, they are often the first to say, "I'll go!"

How about you? What do you do when somebody gives you a job to do? Do you feel sorry for yourself, or do you get started on it right away?

• Responsibility is good training for leaders of character. We need to be the kind of leaders who are eager to take on responsibility. Those are the leaders who are useful to others, and whom others can depend upon. If you have made progress in developing the quality of responsibleness, you're on your way to being a leader of character.

Discipline and Sacrifice

We have covered the qualities of discipline and sacrifice in several previous chapters, but a list of the core qualities of principled leaders would not be complete without them. All true leaders adhere to self-imposed limitations on their lives for the purpose of achieving a higher purpose.

Leaders of principle have learned to govern themselves. They exercise self-control without needing to be disciplined externally. As we, too, progress in character development, we will learn to govern and discipline each area of our lives in order to protect it from ethical lapses and prepare it for maximum productivity. We will train ourselves to do this regardless of whether other people are present, and regardless of whether other people ever find out about it.

Many people have a certain awe about those who sacrifice and suffer in order to do extraordinary acts that will aid humanity, or to accomplish a demanding goal. And that awe is translated into inspiration. In this way, as we have seen, sacrifice based on conviction leads to inspiration. And inspiration is what leads other people to join in fulfilling our vision.

PART IV:

Restoring a Culture of Character

12

Integrating Vision and Values

*"Leaders stand for something—vision.
Leaders stand on something—values."*
—Dr. Myles Munroe

A woman was in the process of cleaning out several boxes in her attic that had been stored there for years—ever since she and her husband had moved into their home to accommodate their growing family of four children, who were now adults. Out of the corner of her eye, she noticed a box half-hidden behind the chimney. It was covered with dust and was still taped shut.

I wonder what's in there? she thought. After carefully brushing away the dust, she pulled the yellowed, wrinkled tape off the center groove of the box and opened up the flaps. Inside, she saw several pieces of red cloth, imprinted with an intricate design, wrapped around some unknown objects. Suddenly, a memory flashed into her mind, taking her back three decades, and she instantly remembered what the items in the box were: several jade objects from China that a friend had given her, which she had inherited from her father. The woman had forgotten all about having received them; she had not given them a thought in years.

The next week, she had the items appraised, and she was stunned to find out they were comparable in age and quality to an eighteenth-century jade collection that had been featured on the television program *Antiques Roadshow* several years earlier. The items in that collection had been valued at as much as one million dollars.

A Long-Forgotten Treasure

In many ways, character in our contemporary culture has become like the long-forgotten treasure the woman in the above scenario found inside the dusty box. She hadn't known what a precious heirloom was in her own house, because she'd abandoned it to a corner of her attic for decades. Likewise, our society has increasingly relegated values and moral standards to the "attics" and "basements" of our culture. Many people don't realize what a treasure our society has lost, because it is out of their moral range of vision. The only way character can come back into their line of sight is for them to see a clear manifestation of it in the lives of leaders like you and me. Then, they will be able to recognize the infinitely valuable gift that has been waiting for them all along, so they can receive it and manifest it in their own lives.

It is up to us to initiate the process of restoring character to our culture. Jesus of Nazareth said that "the kingdom of heaven is like a merchant looking for fine pearls. When he found one of great value, he went away and sold everything he had and bought it."[1] Similar to the merchant who sold everything he owned to obtain the pearl "of great value," we need to make the reintroduction and development of character our number one priority.

There must be a rediscovery, reprioritization, and resurgence of character among the leaders of the world's emerging and industrial states alike, so that we can begin to see the restoration of a culture of character in leadership. Teachers, professors, and educational administrators—from grade schools through universities and other institutions of learning—must reprioritize their programs and curriculum to teach students how to develop and refine their character and to understand why character is essential for individuals, communities, and nations.

We need to make the reintroduction and development of character our number one priority.

We must likewise see a commitment among leaders in all fields of endeavor to transform their own conduct, rededicating themselves to high standards and noble values of genuine leadership. Consequently, we need a new breed of leader who will embrace and manifest a culture of accountability—to himself, to his constituency, and, most important, to the Creator Himself, who extended to us the privilege of representing Him as leaders in the earth.

The Intersection of Vision and Values

We could sum up the entire message of this book in the following way: Leaders stand *for* something—vision. Leaders stand *on* something—values. And, of these two elements, values are of higher importance. As we have noted throughout the preceding chapters, if a leader does not have an active commitment to his values, moral standards, principles, discipline, and ethical code, all of his endeavors will be weakened—and may even be nullified. Since character must be our number one priority in leadership, let's review how vision and values are permanently interrelated in the life of a principled leader.

1. Vision Is an Interpretation of Values

Your vision interprets your values in the sense that it reflects and communicates them. For example, suppose your vision is to help young people who are members of gangs that are undermining your community to become engaged in positive activities that will build up the community, instead. Your vision communicates that you value the lives of young people, and that you value improving the quality of life in your community.

Similarly, an organization's vision reflects its corporate values. For instance, suppose the vision of a home-based business was to create exquisitely embroidered garments to sell to specialty stores, the proceeds of which would supplement the family's income. This vision communicates that that the business, through its owner, values creativity, quality, enterprise, and financial stability.

Therefore, when leaders in politics, religion, education, business, economics, sports, and other fields invest their time and money in a vision, that vision can be used as a measure for assessing their principal values. Jesus of Nazareth said, "For where your treasure is, there your heart will be also."[2]

2. Vision Is Protected by Values

Your vision is only as safe as the values that undergird it. If you cherish a great vision but don't value the principles that would enable you to realize it, you may as well not pursue that vision. There needs to be a marriage of purpose and principles. You have to *know* your purpose, but you must *live* by your principles. In this sense, vision may be compared to the head, and values to the heart. We should take the advice of an ancient proverb that says, "Above all else, guard your heart, for it is the wellspring of life."[3]

It has been said that "the process is as important as the product," and this is certainly true in regard to fulfilling one's vision. Years ago, my organization decided to construct a large building called the Diplomat Center. I envisioned how it would be used to teach people about their purpose as leaders. So, I was excited about it, and I was caught up with securing the property, raising the money, and working long hours to see it come to fruition. However, one day, I sensed that God was saying to me, "I am not pleased with you." I was confused, so I asked, "What are You talking about? I'm doing Your will. You told me to build the building." He said, "You're not leading the people. You are driving them." It broke my heart to realize that I had been driving the people who were involved in the vision, rather than inspiring them.

Then, I felt God saying, "You have passion, and passion is good, but you have no *com*passion. Stop everything. I want you to get your balance back." Deeply convicted, I went into a brief season of solitude in order to regain the balance between my passion and my compassion. The people in my organization were supposed to love this project, not just endure it. So, after reflecting on the situation, I had to go to the people and publicly ask them to forgive me for breaking the law of compassion. I explained to them that, from that point on, we would work together. My confession changed the whole spirit of the organization. People donated more money toward the project, and they also dedicated their time and their skills to see it accomplished.

The ethical issue I had to deal with was that I had been standing *for* something—the idea of how the new building would support the organization's vision—but I hadn't been standing *on* the values that were needed for the process of carrying it out. Having character, therefore, requires more than discovering what you were born to do and pursuing the fulfillment of your vision; it involves pursuing the fulfillment of your vision in a way that corresponds with ethical principles.

Individual leaders and organizations alike should protect themselves against ethical breaches by setting strong values for themselves. For example, an organization's governing board should decide what types of policies it will and will not sanction. A business should determine what standards it will not compromise on. A family should decide what media content it will and will not allow into its home. A corporate entity that has not established values for itself lacks moral protection. It is like a city without walls from ancient times that has left itself vulnerable to deadly attack by enemy armies.

Having character involves pursuing the fulfillment of your vision in a way that corresponds with ethical principles.

Vision Without Values—a False Attempt at Reaching Destiny

When a leader pursues his vision without having established values, he is attempting to reach his destiny without the necessary component of discipline. For example, regardless of how great a leader's vision might be—whether it is to build a family, a church, a business, or a country—the entire process must be balanced by clear, strong values that guide his conduct. As we have seen, no matter how wonderful your anticipated destiny might be, if you don't have discipline, you will short-circuit that destiny and be in danger of losing it completely.

One of my close friends is a distinguished gentleman named Dr. Richard Demeritte Jr. He and I met years ago when he was the ambassador to England from the Bahamas. He has also served as the ambassador to the European Union. When we were talking together one time, he told me a time-honored value his father had conveyed to him: "When in doubt, do what's right." This statement provides extremely valuable yet easy-to-remember ethical advice. When you are faced with a moral choice, just do what's right! A leader of character should always live that way.

The Power of Character to Create Leaders of Principle

In the introduction to this book, we examined principles that showed how crucial leaders are to the development and well-being of a culture. For instance, we noted that nothing advances without leadership and nothing is corrected without leadership. Let's now review what we've learned about the importance of character to the development of leaders equipped to help bring about a cultural course correction and to advance our societies through ethical principles.

1. Character Gives Leaders Credibility

The only avenue for gaining credibility with people so that they will respect our leadership is to develop genuine character. When we demonstrate character, people will not only make deposits in our "trust account," but they will also advance us "credit" as an investment in our future. They will follow us in faith—and every deposit and investment they make will strengthen the credibility of our character. If we continue to be consistent, they will keep following us. We must build a stable and honorable life if we want people to believe what we say about ourselves and our vision. How committed are you to leading with credibility?

2. Character Gives Leaders Moral Force

Character—not power—is the force of true leadership. If a person has moral force, he doesn't need to put physical or emotional pressure on people to make them do what he wants. The moral force of a leader is potent because it has the capacity to influence others.

When you develop into a person of strong character—dependable and stable—that is when you become a true force in leadership. For example, your followers may be deeply impressed by your ability to stay steady under pressure. Consequently, your very presence will bring peace to them, because they will know they can rely on you. People will be influenced by you when they are inspired by you, and inspiration comes from character. Are you focused on power—or on moral force?

"It is curious that physical courage should be so common in the world and moral courage so rare."
—Mark Twain

---

3. Character Ensures That Leaders Maintain Trustworthiness

Trust is a privilege given to the leader by his followers; therefore, a leader must maintain that trust over time and keep it up-to-date. Some companies will spend billions of dollars to protect the longevity of their good name and reputation after a defect or malfunction is discovered in one of their products. They issue a recall and may develop advertising campaigns to alert and reassure their customers, even though doing so entails tremendous cost.

For example, if a toy company hears that a child has gotten hurt because of a defect in one of its products, it will recall the toy, and it will refund its customers in full. To maintain its character, it will spend money to help rectify its mistake. I remember a particular recall of meat due to contamination by E. coli bacteria. The company that supplied the meat immediately stopped its sale, at a loss of likely millions of dollars. But it wasn't too high a price to pay to protect its good name and prevent additional sickness and potential death among its customers.

So, if many companies will go to that kind of effort to protect the integrity of their name in the marketplace, why do many leaders fail to protect the integrity of their names among their followers by ignoring ethical principles? We can't set a price tag on having a good name. Are you willing to pay the costs of self-control, discipline, and delayed gratification in order to establish and maintain true character?

4. Character Legitimizes Leaders

It is character that gives people a legitimate right to lead others. Leaders without character are "illegal," because they are asking people to place their faith in an untrustworthy source. No one has a right to lead if he cannot be trusted, and it would be inappropriate for him to ask people to follow him. If he does, it's as if he is running a scam, because con men are individuals who ask people to trust them, even though they will never deliver what they promise, but will, instead, steal something from them. There are many people throughout our world today who are powerful con men—but they call themselves "leaders."

Is that statement too harsh? I don't think so, because leaders without character who violate people's faith inevitably take away some quantity of their valuable personal assets—things like trust, security, peace of mind, and hope. This is why, when people become disappointed over the poor ethical conduct of a leader they have followed, many of them become angry. They take it personally, because they have committed much of themselves to the leader and his vision. The leader's conduct and its aftereffects constitute a major abuse of the great gifts the people have invested—their time, energy, talents, resources, and commitment—which they have poured out based on their trust.

For example, suppose someone has been a member of a particular church for ten years, bringing her children to Sunday school to be taught good principles, and donating generous financial support. If it were then disclosed that the church's pastor was having an extramarital affair with another member of the congregation, this church member might not only be shocked but also very angry, thinking, *How could he have done that to my money, my time, my children!* She takes it personally because she has invested valuable aspects of her life in the church based on the leader's presumed character. But his conduct canceled the legitimacy of his leadership. Depending on how the other leaders at the church handle the matter, she may feel that she can no longer stay a member of that congregation.

As we have seen, many people today respond to leaders based on what they promise more than on what they value. We need to shift the condition of our support from promises to proven character. The condition should be: "Don't just tell me what you can do for me—show me who you really are. If you clearly demonstrate that you have character, I will give you my trust."

How about you? When people place their faith in you as a leader, are they relying on a trustworthy source—or an untrustworthy one?

5. Character Establishes Integrity in Leaders

We have learned that character is built through tests over time and that having integrity involves the integration of one's thoughts, words, and actions. Thus, a leader's integrity can be established only over the course of time, which allows for this integration to occur. For this reason, leadership should not be given to people who have not yet been tested and tried. They must have a clear history of experiences as evidence that they have demonstrated stability, trustworthiness, and competence over time.

An emerging leader, therefore, must be tested to see if he can stand up under pressure: How stable is he when circumstances are not going well? Can he handle the weight of disappointments? To this end, an individual who is young or untried should be given responsibility gradually, so that he can develop and manifest character with each level of accountability. This principle is the reason I emphasized the core character quality of responsibleness in the previous chapter. If a person does not develop this quality, he cannot become a principled leader. I give many people in my organization challenging responsibilities because I want them to be able to grow and become qualified to accept leadership positions. Therefore, it's important for us not only to build our own character, and not only to look for demonstrated character in other leaders, but also to help our followers develop their character so they may become trusted leaders, as well.

Leadership should not be given to people who have not yet been tested and tried.

Vision Gives Meaning to People...

Many leaders think that their goal should be to get people to believe in them. On the contrary, the goal of leaders should be to get people to believe in *themselves*—to provide an avenue through which they can discover meaning for their lives and manifest their purpose through their personal vision. Helping people to do this requires balance on the part of the leader, because, when people are inspired by a leader's passion, they often confuse the vision with the leader in their minds. In this way, they think they are being drawn to the person. As we have seen, a leader of principle takes the focus off of himself and puts it on the vision. It is the vision—not the leader—that gives people meaning. And it is the vision that will sustain the people's conviction, because that is where they will find their significance in serving their gift to others.

What we have just discussed shows how important it is for us as leaders to act on our convictions and not neglect our vision. When we pursue our own purpose, we actually help other people to find theirs. We should reflect on that responsibility, because the opposite scenario can also occur. Think about it: If we don't maintain our passion for our vision, the people may also lose their energy for their vision. When we feel like giving up and start talking about quitting, the people may also begin to lose their sense of purpose. When we lose our focus, or our commitment to strong character, the people may lose their way in life. Therefore, we must keep vision and values prominent in our lives—other people are depending on us! Who are you currently helping to find meaning and purpose for their own lives through your vision?

...and Values Preserve That Vision

It is imperative that people stay focused on the vision rather than on the leader, because of the danger that a cult of personality will develop. You must never allow people to become so attached to you that they begin to idolize you. How many organizations today have become defunct because they were run by leaders who were "worshipped" by their followers, so that everything fell apart when the leaders had a major moral failure? Leaders need to watch their pride in this respect, because pride can destroy them and their vision. Pride is what makes leaders think they *should* be idolized. They being to think the vision is all about them, that it's built around them, that its success is all up to them.

Let us guard against such attitudes. If we don't want to be humiliated by failure, then we should volunteer right now to humble ourselves. As I emphasized in the previous chapter, humility is another core quality of principled leaders. Cultivating an attitude of humility will help leaders protect themselves and their vision.

Never forget that you and your vision have great significance. "Your" people—the people who are associated with your vision, or will be associated with it—need you. Your character is vital to them. For their sake, as well as your own, commit to be a leader of principle.

A New Beginning for Character

The purpose of this book has been to introduce you to yourself—to your intrinsic significance and your character alike. I want history to write a good account of your life on earth. Please don't become one of those leaders who begins well and starts a good work, only to have a moral failure or become sidetracked before reaching his destiny. Instead, be a great leader who stays true to his convictions and fulfills his purpose and vision according to strong values; one who never betrays the followers who have placed their trust in him.

You have learned many principles and guidelines for character in these pages. But knowledge and understanding of character and its principles are not enough. If we do not act on what we know, it is the equivalent of never having learned it. These principles won't operate in our lives unless we apply them. It is by applying them that we have access to the power of character in leadership. At the back of this book are Character Development Worksheets that will help you to evaluate your current beliefs, convictions, values, moral standards, and discipline, so that you can become intentional about the development of your character.

Perhaps you were not raised with much instruction in morals and ethics. If that is the case, you have likely struggled with character issues that now affect multiple areas of your life—your relationships with other people, your job, and the pursuit of your personal purpose. Because a foundation of character was not established in your life at an early age, you didn't have the resources and wisdom to deal with the various ethical issues you encountered once you reached your teenage years and beyond. I encourage you to use this book as a new beginning for the establishment of strong character in your life.

Principles of character won't operate in our lives unless we apply them.

May we all dedicate ourselves to a new beginning for character—in our own lives, in our families, in our communities, and in our nations. I encourage you to share these principles of character with your children and other family members, your friends, your staff, and your colleagues. The power of character needs to be taught in the halls of government and the boardrooms of every country in the world. No leader should enter into politics, business, education, economics, education, religion, the arts, professional sports, or any other realm until he has established personal moral standards. I believe that ethical principles should be included in premarital counseling courses, as well, to encourage new husbands and wives to become principled leaders who build their homes upon the strong and enduring foundation of character.

Doing nothing about the crisis of character in our world is not an option, because the future of leadership and our culture is at stake—and the world will not transform itself. Our Creator established character as the foundation of human leadership and success. Let us make a lasting commitment to stand *on* vision and to stand *for* values.

How to "Fall Up":
Restoration After Character Failure

The streets of history are littered with the remains of wasted lives— the lives of powerful, talented, skillful, and educated leaders who collapsed under the weight of their achievements, success, notoriety, influence, and power because they lacked an ethical foundation that could have carried them to their destiny. Many of these onetime great leaders undervalued the priority and power of character in their lives. They traded faith for fame, principles for power, and moral respect for reputation.

It is tragic to observe the dishonorable descent of such leaders who, by their own indiscretion, irresponsibility, lack of discipline, and abuse of privilege sell their integrity for temporary pleasures and destroy their character. Sadly, I have personally known and observed many leaders, with great potential to impact the world for good and make a difference in their generation, disintegrate right before my eyes as their outstanding leadership talent and skills dissolved in the murky waters of a life without noble character. Many of them believed that their past accomplishments, achievements, and reputations could compensate for the trust they had lost, but they were greatly mistaken.

Human beings are thus prone to succumb to the lure of power, fame, notoriety, and the adulation of the masses, and many people fall in disgrace by neglecting to secure a strong, durable character. Consequently, we need to ask the following questions: Can a leader survive and recover from a character failure? Is there a way back to the road of leadership success?

Leaders are normally trained in how to succeed, but they are rarely taught how to fail effectively—by learning from their mistakes and making changes to avoid repeating them in the future. They fall down, but they don't know how to "fall up" after failing.

When a leader fails, he is often rejected by those whom he has been leading because of this breach of faith. Although a leader's legacy can be dismantled by defective character, one of the greatest tragedies in the world is when someone with tremendous potential fails morally and then feels he can never be restored. Failing in leadership is not as grave as failing to deal with that failure effectively. If you've fallen, you must make personal changes that will enable you to "fall up," transforming your life from the inside out.

Remember that a leader's ability to function successfully in his role of influencing others for a great cause in the interest of humanity is what I call the "trust factor." Trust is the currency of true leadership and is the power that is deposited into the leader's influence account. The only way to protect this deposit of trust is to establish strong character. If an individual wants to secure his leadership, he must make protecting and maintaining his account of trust his principal responsibility. It can take years for a leader to build this account—but only minutes of irresponsibility to deplete it and even cancel it.

The following are the steps to restoration, reconciliation, and reclamation after you have experienced a moral failure or otherwise "fallen" in your leadership role:

1. Admit your need for help.

2. Confess your violation of trust.

3. Identify a true and reliable authority in your life to be accountable to.

4. Practice complete submission to that authority without condition.

5. Obey the advice, counsel, and instruction of that authority without condition.

6. Accept full responsibility for your fall.

7. Agree never to attempt to defend yourself or your act of indiscretion.

8. Agree to allow the authority to represent and speak on your behalf to your constituency and the greater community.

9. Practice total submission to the discretion of the authority with regard to your readiness to return to public service.

10. Establish a permanent relationship with the authority for the purpose of ongoing accountability.

If a leader follows these steps, he can find healing and restoration. The safest course to take when you fall is to submit yourself to a qualified human authority.

Again, failure is not the termination of a leader's call, assignment, gifts, or talents. It must be seen as a detour, an interruption, and even an attempt to cancel destiny. If you have fallen down, it's time for you to "fall up" and seek restoration.

Make sure you take time out from your other responsibilities to evaluate what went wrong. Some leaders who fail keep on going as if nothing had happened. You will need to seek forgiveness from those you have let down, but then you must develop self-control, steadiness, maturity, and all the other values of principled leadership. Trust the Creator to restore you to leadership when you are ready for it. There is life after "the fall," but you must follow the process of restoration in order to receive its benefits.

Notes

Introduction

1. S. E. Cupp, "Why the AP Scandal Is So Scary," *The New York Daily News*, May 21, 2013, http://www.nydailynews.com/opinion/ap-scandal-scary-article-1.1349443; Mark Hosenball, "Attorney General Signed Off on Fox Phone Records Subpoena: Sources," Reuters, May 28, 2013, http://news.yahoo.com/news-corp-denies-having-record-fox-news-subpoena-061749426.html.

2. Timothy B. Lee, "Everything You Need to Know About the NSA Scandal," June 6, 2013, http://www.washingtonpost.com/blogs/wonkblog/wp/2013/06/06/everything-you-need-to-know-about-the-nsa-scandal.

3. "The Iran-Contra Affair," *American Experience*, PBS, http://www.pbs.org/wgbh/americanexperience/features/general-article/reagan-iran/; "Iran-Contra Affair," *Encyclopaedia Britannica*, http://www.britannica.com/EBchecked/topic/293519/Iran-Contra-Affair.

4. "Brazil to Investigate Ex-President Lula in Vote-Buying Scandal," Reuters, April 6, 2013, http://uk.reuters.com/article/2013/04/06/uk-brazil-lula-probe-idUKBRE93507B20130406.

5. "Uhuru Kenyatta Trial Moved to November," BBC, June 20, 2013, http://www.bbc.co.uk/news/world-africa-22985456; Patrick McGroarty, "Court Aims to Prove Case in Africa," *The Wall Street Journal*, May 30, 2013, page 12.

6. Patrick McGroarty, "Court Aims to Prove Case in Africa," *The Wall Street Journal*, May 30, 2013, page 12.

7. "U.N. War-Crimes Tribunal Convicts 6 Bosnian Croats," Associated Press, reported in *The Wall Street Journal*, May 30, 2013, page 6.

8. "Manuel Noriega," *The New York Times*, July 7, 2010, http://topics.nytimes.com/top/reference/timestopics/people/n/manuel_antonio_noriega/index.html; "Noriega Swaps Prison in France for Jail in Panama," http://www.euronews.com/2011/12/11/panama-s-former-dictator-manuel-noriega-is-returning-to-his-home-country-but-/; Randal C. Archibold, "Noriega Is Sent to Prison Back in Panama, Where the Terror Has Turned to Shrugs," *The New York Times*, December 11, 2011, http://www.nytimes.com/2011/12/12/world/americas/noriega-back-in-panama-for-more-prison-time.html?_r=0.

9. Maureen Farrell, "JPMorgan Settles Electricity Manipulation Case for $410 Million," July 30, 2013, http://money.cnn.com/2013/07/30/investing/jp-morgan-electricity-fines/index.html.

10. Michael Ono, "8 High-Profile Financial Scandals in 5 Months," ABC News, August 17, 2012, abcnews.go.com/Business/high-profile-financial-scandals-months/story?id=17023140.
11. Steven Mufson, "Did Halliburton Cut a Good Deal with Justice?" *The Washington Post* with Bloomberg, July 26, 2013, http://articles.washingtonpost.com/2013-07-26/business/40864106_1_oil-spill-criminal-charges-justice-department; "Gulf Oil Spill: Halliburton to Plead Guilty to Destroying Evidence," Reuters, http://www.theguardian.com/business/2013/jul/26/halliburton-destroying-gulf-oil-evidence.
12. "SEC Charges KBR and Halliburton for FCPA Violations," SEC Press Release, February 11, 2009, http://www.sec.gov/news/press/2009/2009-23.htm.
13. Clifford Krauss, "Halliburton Pleads Guilty to Destroying Evidence After Gulf Spill," *The New York Times*, July 25, 2013, http://www.nytimes.com/2013/07/26/business/halliburton-pleads-guilty-to-destroying-evidence-after-gulf-spill.html?_r=0&gwh=65AB95E080DB9BBB40E6A023562D46EA.
14. Tom Shroder, "Halliburton's Guilt Doesn't Absolve BP," July 26, 2013, http://gcaptain.com/halliburtons-guilt-doesnt-absolve-bp/.
15. Sital S. Patel, "Madoff: Don't Let Wall Street Scam You, like I Did," MarketWatch.com, *The Wall Street Journal*, http://www.marketwatch.com/story/madoff-dont-let-wall-street-scam-you-like-i-did-2013-06-05.
16. Diana B. Henriques, "Madoff Is Sentenced to 150 Years for Ponzi Scheme, *The New York Times*, June 29, 2009, http://www.nytimes.com/2009/06/30/business/30madoff.html?pagewanted=all&_r=0; http://www.justice.gov/usao/nys/madoff/20090629sentencingtranscriptcorrected.pdf.
17. Victor Simpson and Nicole Winfield, "Vatican Bank Hit by Financial Scandal...Again," December 19, 2010, http://www.independent.co.uk/news/world/europe/vatican-bank-hit-by-financial-scandal-again-2164321.html; Carol Matlack, "A Money-Smuggling Scandal Threatens to Sink the Vatican Bank," July 2, 2013, http://www.businessweek.com/articles/2013-07-02/a-money-smuggling-scandal-threatens-to-sink-the-vatican-bank.
18. Independent Commission Against Corruption, www.icac.org.hk/newsl/issue2/carrien.html; http://www.icac.org.hk/new_icac/eng/cases/carrian/carrian.html; http://en.wikipedia.org/wiki/List_of_corporate_collapses_and_scandals.
19. Louise Armitstead, "Debt Crisis: Greek Government Signs €330m Settlement with Siemens," *The Telegraph*, August 27, 2012, http://www.telegraph.co.uk/finance/financialcrisis/9502146/Debt-crisis-Greek-government-signs-330m-settlement-with-Siemens.html.
20. David Teather, "Gap Admits to Child Labour Violations in Outsource Factories," *The Guardian*, May 12, 2004, http://www.theguardian.com/business/2004/may/13/7; http://en.wikipedia.org/wiki/List_of_corporate_collapses_and_scandals.
21. Rebecca Leung, "Battling Big Tobacco," CBSNews.com, February 11, 2009, http://www.cbsnews.com/2100-500164_162-666867.html.
22. Doug Ferguson, "After Scandal and Toughest Year of His Life, Woods Strives to Move Forward," Associated Press, http://www.pga.com/after-scandal-and-toughest-year-life-tiger-woods-strives-move-forward.
23. "Lance Armstrong," http://www.biography.com/people/lance-armstrong-9188901.
24. "Track Star Marion Jones Sentenced to 6 Months," CNN, January 11, 2008, http://www.cnn.com/2008/CRIME/01/11/jones.doping/; "I Did Not Deserve Prison, Says Athlete Marion Jones," December 6, 2010, http://news.bbc.co.uk/sport2/hi/tv_and_radio/inside_sport/9258742.stm.

25. Mark Scolforo, "Jerry Sandusky Moved to Greene State Prison to Serve Sentence," Associated Press, October 31, 2012, http://www.huffingtonpost.com/2012/11/01/jerry-sandusky-greene-state-prison-_n_2056463.html.

26. Rick Weinberg, "ESPN Counts Down the 100 Most Memorable Moments of the Past 25 Years: #5 Pete Rose Banned from Baseball," http://sports.espn.go.com/espn/espn25/story?page=moments/5; Jill Lieber and Steve Wulf, "Sad Ending for a Hero," July 30, 1990, http://sportsillustrated.cnn.com/vault/article/magazine/MAG1136591/.

27. See, for example, "Catholic Church Sex Scandals Around the World," September 14, 2010, http://www.bbc.co.uk/news/10407559; "Roman Catholic Church Sex Abuse Cases," http://topics.nytimes.com/top/reference/timestopics/organizations/r/roman_catholic_church_sex_abuse_cases/index.html.

28. Adelle M. Banks, "Bishop Eddie Long Sued Over Alleged Ponzi Scheme," Religion News Service, February 19, 2013, http://www.huffingtonpost.com/2013/02/19/bishop-eddie-long-sued-over-alleged-ponzi-scheme_n_2713413.html.

29. Gina Meeks, "Eddie Long Sued by Former Church Members over Alleged Ponzi Scheme," February 13, 2013, Charisma News, http://www.charismanews.com/us/38230-eddie-long-sued-by-former-church-members-over-alleged-ponzi-scheme.

30. Shelia M. Poole, "SEC Complaint Alleges That Ponzi Scheme Targeted Church Members," April 12, 2012, *The Atlanta Journal-Constitution*, http://www.ajc.com/news/news/local/sec-complaint-alleges-that-ponzi-scheme-targeted-c/nQSzp/.

31. Joanne Kaufman, "The Fall of Jimmy Swaggart," *People*, March 7, 1988, http://www.people.com/people/archive/article/0,,20098413,00.html.

32. "Jim Bakker Freed From Jail to Stay in a Halfway House," *The New York Times*, July 2, 1994, http://www.nytimes.com/1994/07/02/us/jim-bakker-freed-from-jail-to-stay-in-a-halfway-house.html; Hanna Rosin, "Televangelist Jim Bakker's Road to Redemption," *The Washington Post*, August 11, 1999, http://www.washingtonpost.com/wp-srv/style/daily/aug99/bakker11.htm; Adelle M. Banks, "Jim Baker Starts 45-year Jail Term," *Orlando Sentinel*, October 25, 1989, http://articles.orlandosentinel.com/1989-10-25/news/8910252596_1_jim-bakker-ministry-start-a-prison.

33. "Disgraced Pastor Haggard Admits Second Relationship with Man," January 30, 2009, http://www.cnn.com/2009/US/01/29/lkl.ted.haggard/.

34. Katie Lindelan, "Mel Gibson's Marriage Ends After 28 Years and Beach Embrace Pictures," April 14, 2009, http://www.telegraph.co.uk/news/celebritynews/5151901/Mel-Gibsons-marriage-ends-after-28-years-and-beach-embrace-pictures.html; "Mel Gibson Loses Half of His $850 Million Fortune to Ex-Wife in Divorce," ABC News, December 26, 2011, abcnews.go.com/blogs/entertainment/2011/12/mel-gibsons-loses-half-of-his-850-million-fortune-to-ex-wife-in-divorce/.

35. "Mel Gibson Breaks Silence on Domestic Violence Scandal," Reuters, April 22, 2011, http://www.reuters.com/article/2011/04/22/us-melgibson-idUSTRE73L37G20110422.

36. Margaret Sullivan, "Repairing the Credibility Cracks," *The New York Times*, May 4, 2013, http://www.nytimes.com/2013/05/05/public-editor/repairing-the-credibility-cracks-after-jayson-blair.html?pagewanted=all&_r=0.

37. "Frey Admits Lying; Oprah Apologizes to Viewers," Associated Press, January 27, 2006, http://www.today.com/id/11030647/ns/today-today_books/t/frey-admits-lying-oprah-apologizes-viewers/; "Bending the Truth in a Million Little Ways," *The New York Times*, January 17, 2006, http://www.nytimes.com/2006/01/17/books/17kaku.html?pagewanted=all.

38. "Whitney Houston," http://www.biography.com/people/whitney-houston-9344818?page=3.
39. Matt Volz, "Greg Mortenson, 'Three Cups of Tea' Author, Must Repay Charity $1 Million: Report," April 5, 2012, http://www.huffingtonpost.com/2012/04/05/greg-mortenson-three-cups_n_1407177.html.
40. Greg Mortenson and David Oliver Relin, *Three Cups of Tea: One Man's Mission to Promote Peace…One School at a Time* (New York: Penguin Books, 2006), 4.
41. Jeff Barnard, "'Three Cups of Tea' Co-Author Relin Kills Self," Associated Press, December 3, 2012, http://www.boston.com/ae/celebrity/2012/12/03/three-cups-tea-author-relin-kills-self/KhIWpKTG8TgBkbCnTP7cYJ/story.html; Michael Daly, "The Death of Co-Author of 'Three Cups of Tea' Is Ruled Suicide," The Daily Beast, December 6, 2012, http://www.thedailybeast.com/articles/2012/12/06/the-death-of-co-author-of-three-cups-of-tea-is-ruled-suicide.html.
42. Robert D. McFadden, "William Aramony, 84; Forced Out in United Way Scandal," November 15, 2011, http://www.boston.com/bostonglobe/obituaries/articles/2011/11/15/william_aramony_84_forced_out_in_united_way_scandal/; "William Aramony Dies at 84; United Way Chief Executive," Associated Press, November 15, 2011, http://www.latimes.com/news/obituaries/la-me-william-aramony-20111115,0,1264814.story.
43. "William Aramony Dead at 84," December 1, 2011, *The NonProfit Times*, http://www.thenonprofittimes.com/news-articles/william-aramony-dead-at-84/.
44. Ryan Smith, "Christian Charity Feed the Children Says Frontman Larry Jones Hoarded Porno, Money and Power," December 31, 2009, http://www.cbsnews.com/8301-504083_162-6037886-504083.html.
45. Nolan Clay, "Feed The Children, Fired President Settle Lawsuit," NewsOK, January 30, 2011, http://newsok.com/feed-the-children-fired-president-settle-lawsuit/article/3536442.
46. C. S. Lewis, *The Great Divorce* (New York: HarperCollins, 1946, 1973), viii.

Chapter 1

1. Sentencing transcript, United States District Court, Southern District of New York, June 29, 2009.
2. Proverbs 22:1.
3. "Lunch Ladies In Court, Accused Of Stealing $94K," KDKA news, February 25, 2013, http://pittsburgh.cbslocal.com/2013/02/25/lunch-ladies-in-court-accused-of-stealing-94k/.
4. "Jesse L. Jackson Jr. Sentenced to 30 Months in Prison," *The Washington Post*, August 14, 2013, http://www.washingtonpost.com/local/jesse-l-jackson-jr-set-to-be-sentenced-in-dc-federal-court/2013/08/13/ac5e8296-0452-11e3-88d6-d5795fab4637_story_1.html.
5. Ryan J. Reilly, "Jesse Jackson Jr. Sentenced For Defrauding Campaign," August 14, 2013, http://www.huffingtonpost.com/2013/08/14/jesse-jackson-jr-sentenced_n_3752476.html.
6. Matthew 16:26.

7. Raymund Flandez, "Livestrong Tries to Move Beyond Armstrong Doping Scandal," *The Chronicle of Philanthropy*, February 28, 2013, http://philanthropy.com/article/Livestrong-Tries-to-Move/137621/.
8. Hitendra Wadhwa, "The Wrath of a Great Leader," http://www.inc.com/hitendra-wadhwa/great-leadership-how-martin-luther-king-jr-wrestled-with-anger.html.
9. Diana B. Henriques, "Madoff Is Sentenced to 150 Years for Ponzi Scheme, *The New York Times*, June 29, 2009, http://www.nytimes.com/2009/06/30/business/30madoff.html.
10. Diana B. Henriques and Al Baker, "A Madoff Son Hangs Himself on Father's Arrest Anniversary," December 11, 2010, http://www.nytimes.com/2010/12/12/business/12madoff.html.
11. Carol Kuruvilla, "Andrew Madoff continues battle with stage-four cancer, receives donor lymphocyte infusion," *New York Daily News*, August 9, 2013, http://www.nydailynews.com/new-york/andrew-madoff-continues-battle-stage-four-cancer-article-1.1422947.

Chapter 2

1. Proverbs 18:16 (NKJV).
2. "Notes for a Law Lecture," circa July 1850, quoted in John P. Frank, *Lincoln as a Lawyer* (Urbana: University of Illinois Press, 1961), 35.
3. Editor's note: For more on discovering personal leadership and gifting, please see *The Principles and Power of Vision* and *The Spirit of Leadership* by Myles Munroe.
4. Lewis Copeland, Lawrence W. Lamm, and Stephen J. McKenna, eds., *The World's Great Speeches* (Mineola, New York: Dover Publications, Inc., 1999), 753.
5. Roy P. Basler, ed., *Abraham Lincoln: His Speeches and Writings*, 2nd ed. (Cambridge, MA: Da Capo Press, 2001), 578.
6. "An Ideal for Which I Am Prepared to Die," April 22, 2007, http://www.theguardian.com/world/2007/apr/23/nelsonmandela.
7. Winston S. Churchill, ed., *Never Give In!: The Best of Winston Churchill's Speeches* (New York: Hyperion, 2003), 229.
8. Numbers 13:33.
9. Dan Bilefsky and Jane Perlez, "Vaclav Havel, Former Czech President, Dies at 75," December 18, 2011, http://www.nytimes.com/2011/12/19/world/europe/vaclav-havel-dissident-playwright-who-led-czechoslovakia-dead-at-75.html.
10. Matthew 15:14.

Chapter 3

1. Proverbs 23:7 (NKJV).

Chapter 4

1. "More Leaders Adopting 'Intimidating' Leadership Style," https://www.leadershipiq.com/white-papers/more-leaders-adopting-intimidator-leadership-style/.

2. Carol Stephenson, "Leaders of Good Character," http://www.iveybusinessjournal.com/departments/from-the-dean/leaders-of-good-character.
3. Matthew 6:33 (NKJV).

Chapter 5

1. Matthew 6:21.
2. Matthew 15:17–19.
3. Hestie Barnard Gerber, "10 Modern-Day Heroes Actively Changing the World," May 31, 2013, http://listverse.com/2013/05/31/10-modern-day-heroes-actively-changing-the-world/.
4. 1 Corinthians 9:24–27 (NIrV).
5. 1 Samuel 24:13.
6. See 1 Samuel 24, 26.
7. Proverbs 1:19.
8. See 2 Samuel 15, 17–18.
9. See 2 Samuel 11.
10. See 2 Samuel 12:1–24; Psalm 51.

Chapter 6

1. Talatu Usman, "Nigeria: 120 Million Nigerians Lack Access to Electricity Supply—Power Minister," June 6, 2013, *Premium Times*, http://allafrica.com/stories/201306060981.html; "Power Minister Says Nigerians Now Enjoy 16 Hours of Electricity Supply," July 23, 2013, Channels Television, http://www.channelstv.com/home/2013/07/23/power-minister-says-nigerians-now-enjoy-16-hours-of-electricity-supply/.
2. http://www.redcross.org/what-we-do/international-services.
3. http://www.rolls-roycemotorcars.com/the-company/.
4. www.fda.gov.
5. www.fdic.gov.
6. www.bbb.org/us/mission-and-values/.
7. http://www.fdic.gov/about/mission/.

Chapter 7

1. http://mlk-kpp01.stanford.edu/primarydocuments/Vol2/540228RediscoveringLostValues.pdf.
2. Luke 6:47–49.
3. Genesis 1:26–27.
4. Merrill F. Unger and William White Jr., eds., "Nelson's Expository Dictionary of the Old Testament," in *Vine's Complete Expository Dictionary of Old and New Testament Words* (Nashville: Thomas Nelson Publishers, 1985), 244.

5. *Strong's Exhaustive Concordance of the Bible*, electronic version, copyright 1980, 1986, and assigned to World Bible Publishers, Inc.
6. Genesis 2:7.
7. "Nelson's Expository Dictionary of the Old Testament," 137.
8. Malachi 3:6.
9. James 1:17–18.
10. Exodus 3:6.
11. Isaiah 44:24.
12. Leviticus 11:45.
13. Psalm 9:16.
14. Exodus 23:1–6.
15. 1 John 4:8, 16.
16. Lamentations 3:22–23.
17. Genesis 1:26 (KJV, NKJV).
18. Genesis 1:26.
19. Genesis 1:28.
20. See Genesis 3.
21. James 3:11–12.
22. James 1:6–8.
23. Matthew 3:17.
24. John 10:30.
25. John 1:1–4, 14.
26. Colossians 2:9.
27. John 3:5.
28. See John 14:6.
29. Mark 1:15.
30. Matthew 20:25–28.

Chapter 8

1. Psalm 119:4.
2. Psalm 119:93.
3. Psalm 2:1–3.
4. Psalm 2:4.
5. Psalm 119:45.
6. Psalm 119:99.
7. Proverbs 6:6–11.
8. Luke 6:41–42.
9. See Genesis 2:16–17.
10. Psalm 119:45.

Chapter 9

1. Hebrews 13:8.
2. See James 1:8.

3. Matthew 13:33.
4. Luke 23:34.
5. See Numbers 14:24.
6. See Genesis 37, 39–41.
7. Genesis 39:9.
8. *Online Etymology Dictionary*, http://www.etymonline.com/index.php?search=hypocrisy.
9. Matthew 6:2.
10. Matthew 23:25.
11. *Churchill: The Life Triumphant*, compiled by *American Heritage Magazine* and United Press International (American Heritage Publishing Co., Inc.), 93.

Chapter 10

1. Romans 5:3–5.
2. *Strong's Exhaustive Concordance of the Bible*, electronic version, copyright 1980, 1986, and assigned to World Bible Publishers, Inc.
3. Hebrews 12:11.
4. Luke 22:33.
5. See Luke 22:31–32.
6. Matthew 4:1.
7. Matthew 4:2–10.
8. James 1:13–14.
9. 3 John 2 (NKJV).
10. See, for example, Exodus 20:15; Romans 13:9.

Chapter 11

1. Genesis 41:15.
2. Genesis 41:16.
3. Proverbs 29:25.
4. See, for example, Matthew 25:21, 23.
5. Genesis 41:39–41.
6. Genesis 41:46–49.

Chapter 12

1. Matthew 13:45–46.
2. Matthew 6:21.
3. Proverbs 4:23.

Character Development Worksheets

We have covered in close detail the building blocks of solid character and the process by which they are developed in the life of a leader with integrity. We have examined the various steps of the progression from beliefs to convictions, to values, to morals/principles, to discipline, to ethics, and, finally, to a lifestyle that reflects sound character. But all of these principles will remain mere words on a page until you apply them to your own situation—until you think through your personal set of beliefs and values, articulate the resulting convictions you hold, and explore the degree to which your behavior reflects them. Only through honest, objective self-assessment will you arrive at a true picture of your character, as it is now, so that you may plan how to refine it into the character you ought to have.

The following pages provide an opportunity for you to do just that. Each of the worksheets poses a prompt to promote self-reflection, as well as room to write out your responses, so that you may refer to them later and remind yourself of what you have committed to stand for.

Beliefs

What Are Some of My
Foundational Beliefs and Guiding Principles?
(See pages 69–73.)

+ Example: *"It is more blessed to give than to receive."* (Acts 20:35)

+ Example: *Every person on earth is intrinsically valuable and deserves to be given respect and justice.*

+ _____

_____

+ _____

_____

+ _____

_____

+ _____

_____

+ _____

_____

- _____

  _____

- _____

  _____

- _____

  _____

- _____

  _____

- _____

  _____

- _____

  _____

Convictions

What Are Some Strong Convictions Based on My Beliefs?
(See pages 54–55, 73.)

+ Example: *I have a responsibility to help relieve the needs of people who lack food, water, and shelter.*

+ _____

_____

+ _____

_____

+ _____

_____

+ _____

_____

+ _____

_____

+ _____

Values

*On What Ideas, Principles, and Qualities Do I Personally
Place High Worth?*
(See pages 82–89.)

✦ Example: *I value the quality of generosity.*

✦ _____

_____

✦ _____

_____

✦ _____

_____

✦ _____

_____

✦ _____

_____

✦ _____

Moral Standards

What Are My Personal Principles for Living?
(See pages 99–103.)

+ Example: *Because I value generosity, one of my personal moral standards, or principles for living, is to give a certain percentage of my monthly income toward meeting the material needs of others.*

+ _____

_____

+ _____

_____

+ _____

_____

+ _____

_____

+ _____

_____

+ _____

Discipline

How Does My Conduct Reflect the Priorities I Have Chosen to
Direct My Vision and My Lifestyle?
(See pages 103–106.)

+   Example: *To fulfill my personal principle of giving a certain percentage of my monthly income to meet other people's material needs, I eat out at expensive restaurants only when celebrating a very special occasion, such as occurs once or twice a year.*

+   _____

_____

+   _____

_____

+   _____

_____

+   _____

_____

+   _____

_____

For Personal Reflection

How Much Do I Value the Following?

- God
- Marriage
- Family
- Children
- Friends
- Love
- Forgiveness
- Money
- Power
- Influence
- Sex
- Transparency
- Honesty
- Truthfulness
- Courage

- Sincerity
- Self-esteem
- Self-respect
- Caring
- Thoughtfulness
- Kindness
- Compassion
- Tolerance
- Courtesy
- Cooperation
- Patience
- Teachable
- Loyalty
- Humility
- Service

Personal Character Contract

- Write a contract with yourself that establishes your personal VALUES STATEMENT and CODE OF ETHICS by which you commit to live in the exercise of your personal and public leadership responsibilities.

- Give a copy of this contract to two trusted friends who will hold you accountable for keeping your life Character Contract.

About the Author

D r. Myles Munroe is an international motivational speaker, best-selling author, educator, leadership mentor, and consultant for government and business. Traveling extensively throughout the world, Dr. Munroe addresses critical issues affecting the full range of human, social, and spiritual development. The central theme of his message is the maximization of individual potential, including the transformation of followers into leaders and leaders into agents of change.

Dr. Munroe is founder and president of Bahamas Faith Ministries International (BFMI), a multidimensional organization headquartered in Nassau, Bahamas. He is chief executive officer and chairman of the board of the International Third World Leaders Association and president of the International Leadership Training Institute.

Dr. Munroe is also the founder and executive producer of a number of radio and television programs aired worldwide. In addition, he is a frequent quest on other television and radio programs and international networks and is a contributing writer for various Bible editions, journals, magazines, and newsletters, such as *The Believer's Topical Bible, The African Cultural Heritage Topical Bible, Charisma Life Christian Magazine,* and *Ministries Today.* He is a popular author of more than forty books, including *The Purpose and Power of Authority, The Principles and Benefits of Change, Becoming a Leader, The Most Important Person on Earth, The Spirit of Leadership, The Principles and Power of Vision, Understanding the Purpose and Power of Prayer, Understanding the Purpose and Power of Woman,* and *Understanding the Purpose and Power of Men.* Dr. Munroe has changed the lives of multitudes around the world with a powerful message that inspires, motivates, challenges, and empowers people to discover personal purpose, develop true potential, and manifest their unique leadership abilities. For over thirty years, he has trained tens of thousands of leaders in business, industry, education, government, and religion. He personally addresses over 500,000 people each year on personal and professional development. His appeal and message transcend age, race, culture, creed, and economic background.

Dr. Munroe has earned B.A. and M.A. degrees from Oral Roberts University and the University of Tulsa, and he has been awarded a number of honorary doctoral degrees. He has also served as an adjunct professor of the Graduate School of Theology at Oral Roberts University.

Dr. Munroe and his wife, Ruth, travel as a team and are involved in teaching seminars together. Both are leaders who minister with sensitive hearts and international vision. They are the proud parents of two adult children, Charisa and Chairo (Myles Jr.).